THE WAY
PEOPLE
LIVE

Life on the
Oregon Trail

Titles in The Way People Live series include:

Cowboys in the Old West
Life Among the Great Plains Indians
Life Among the Ibo Women of Nigeria
Life Among the Indian Fighters
Life Among the Pirates
Life Among the Samurai
Life Among the Vikings
Life During the Crusades
Life During the French Revolution
Life During the Gold Rush
Life During the Great Depression
Life During the Middle Ages
Life During the Renaissance
Life During the Russian Revolution
Life During the Spanish Inquisition
Life in a Japanese American Internment Camp
Life in Ancient Greece
Life in Ancient Rome
Life in an Eskimo Village
Life in a Wild West Show
Life in Charles Dickens's England
Life in the Amazon Rain Forest
Life in the American Colonies
Life in the Elizabethan Theater
Life in the North During the Civil War
Life in the South During the Civil War
Life in the Warsaw Ghetto
Life in War-Torn Bosnia
Life of a Roman Slave
Life on a Medieval Pilgrimage
Life on an Israeli Kibbutz
Life on the American Frontier
Life on the Oregon Trail

THE WAY PEOPLE LIVE

Life on the Oregon Trail

by Gary L. Blackwood

Lucent Books, P.O. Box 289011, San Diego, CA 92198-9011

Library of Congress Cataloging-in-Publication Data

Blackwood, Gary L.
    Life on the Oregon Trail / by Gary L. Blackwood
        p.   cm. — (The way people live)
    Includes bibliographical references (p.   ) and index.
    ISBN 1-56006-540-0 (lib. : alk. paper)
    1. Oregon Trail—Juvenile literature. 2. Pioneers—Oregon Trail—
Social life and customs—Juvenile literature. 3. Frontier and pioneer
life—West (U.S.)—Juvenile literature. 4. Overland journeys to the Pacific—
Juvenile literature. I. Title. II. Series.
    F880.B56   1999
    979.5—dc21   98-48958
                                                                               CIP
                                                                               AC

CURR (handwritten margin note)

Contents

Discovering the Humanity in Us All

The Way People Live series focuses on pockets of human culture. Some of these are current cultures, like the Eskimos of the Arctic; others no longer exist, such as the Jewish ghetto in Warsaw during World War II. What many of these cultural pockets share, however, is the fact that they have been viewed before, but not completely understood.

To really understand any culture, it is necessary to strip the mind of the common notions we hold about groups of people. These stereotypes are the archenemies of learning. It does not even matter whether the stereotypes are positive or negative; they are confining and tight. Removing them is a challenge that's not easily met, as anyone who has ever tried it will admit. Ideas that do not fit into the templates we create are unwelcome visitors—ones we would prefer remain quietly in a corner or forgotten room.

The cowboy of the Old West is a good example of such confining roles. The cowboy was courageous, yet soft-spoken. His time (it is always a he, in our template) was spent alternatively saving a rancher's daughter from certain death on a runaway stagecoach, or shooting it out with rustlers. At times, of course, he was likely to get a little crazy in town after a trail drive, but for the most part, he was the epitome of inner strength. It is disconcerting to find out that the cowboy is human, even a bit childish. Can it really be true that cowboys would line up to help the cook on the trail drive grind coffee, just hoping he would give them a little stick of pep-

permint candy that came with the coffee shipment? The idea of tough cowboys vying with one another to help "Coosie" (as they called their cooks) for a bit of candy seems silly and out of place.

So is the vision of Eskimos playing video games and watching MTV, living in prefab housing in the Arctic. It just does not fit with what "Eskimo" means. We are far more comfortable with snow igloos and whale blubber, harpoons and kayaks.

Although the cultures dealt with in Lucent's The Way People Live series are often historically and socially well known, the emphasis is on the personal aspects of life. Groups of people, while unquestionably affected by their politics and their governmental structures, are more than those institutions. How do people in a particular time and place educate their children? What do they eat? And how do they build their houses? What kinds of work do they do? What kinds of games do they enjoy? The answers to these questions bring these cultures to life. People's lives are revealed in the particulars and only by knowing the particulars can we understand these cultures' will to survive and their moments of weakness and greatness.

This is not to say that understanding politics does not help to understand a culture. There is no question that the Warsaw ghetto, for example, was a culture that was brought about by the politics and social ideas of Adolf Hitler and the Third Reich. But the Jews who were crowded together in the ghetto cannot be understood by the Reich's politics. Their life was a day-to-day battle for existence, and the creativity and methods they used to prolong their lives is a vital story of human perseverance that would be denied by focusing only on the institutions of Hitler's Germany. Knowing that children as young as five or six outwitted Nazi guards on a daily basis, that Jewish policemen helped the Germans control the ghetto, that children attended secret schools in the ghetto and even earned diplomas—these are the things that reveal the fabric of life, that can inspire, intrigue, and amaze.

Books in The Way People Live series allow both the casual reader and the student to see humans as victims, heroes, and onlookers. And although humans act in ways that can fill us with feelings of sorrow and revulsion, it is important to remember that "hero," "predator," and "victim" are dangerous terms. Heaping undue pity or praise on people reduces them to objects, and strips them of their humanity.

Seeing the Jews of Warsaw only as victims is to deny their humanity. Seeing them only as they appear in surviving photos, staring at the camera with infinite sadness, is limiting, both to them and to those who want to understand them. To an object of pity, the only appropriate response becomes "Those poor creatures!" and that reduces both the quality of their struggle and the depth of their despair. No one is served by such two-dimensional views of people and their cultures.

With this in mind, The Way People Live series strives to flesh out the traditional, two-dimensional views of people in various cultures and historical circumstances. Using a wide variety of primary quotations—the words not only of the politicians and government leaders, but of the real people whose lives are being examined—each book in the series attempts to show an honest and complete picture of a culture removed from our own by time or space.

By examining cultures in this way, the reader will notice not only the glaring differences from his or her own culture, but also will be struck by the similarities. For indeed, people share common needs—warmth, good company, stability, and affirmation from others. Ultimately, seeing how people really live, or have lived, can only enrich our understanding of ourselves.

Agents of Manifest Destiny

The vast majority of men and women who crossed the continent on the Oregon Trail in the mid-1800s did so for purely personal reasons. They were looking for a less crowded and more fertile place to farm, or they dreamed of getting rich in the goldfields, or they planned to make money selling trade goods. Yet, unknown to most of them, they were all a part of a grander scheme called Manifest Destiny.

Journalist John L. Sullivan coined the term in 1845, in an editorial that called for the United States to annex Texas. It was, Sullivan wrote, our country's "manifest destiny to overspread the continent allotted by Providence for the free development of our yearly multiplying millions." [1]

Sullivan was one of a sizable number of writers, politicians, and ordinary citizens who called themselves "expansionists." The more extreme among them believed that the United States had a God-given right to occupy all of North America from the Atlantic to the Pacific—and perhaps much of the rest of the world as well. The more moderate were willing to settle for everything between Canada and the Rio Grande.

A wagon train of Mormons pulling handcarts crosses the Great Plains.

Virginia congressman John Floyd expressed very clearly the motivation that lay behind this belief:

> With two oceans washing our shores, commercial wealth is ours and imagination can hardly conceive the greatness, the grandeur, the power that await us.[2]

Expanding America

The country had taken a major step toward this goal in 1803, when the government purchased the vast Louisiana Territory from France. But large parts of the North American continent were still in the hands of Mexico and England. The expansionists were eager to claim what was left.

As early as 1818 the American government proposed that a boundary between Canada and the United States be drawn at the forty-ninth parallel, granting the United States all of what is now Oregon and Washington. Many felt that America had a solid claim to the area, since a U.S. vessel, the *Columbia*, had been the first to sail up and explore—and give a name to—the Columbia River.

But the British had been conducting a lucrative fur trade out of their base at Fort Vancouver for many years, and they were reluctant to give up the area. Eventually they agreed to accept the American proposal for three main reasons: The fur trade was dwindling. Also, since ardent expansionists such as President James K. Polk were clamoring to draw the boundary even farther north, at 54° 40', the British naturally preferred the earlier terms. Lastly, in 1841, emigrants from the United States had begun pouring into Oregon Country, first in a trickle and then in a steady stream. Though on paper the new land still belonged equally to England and the United States, it had become for all practical purposes American territory.

In 1848 Oregon officially became a territory of the United States. By then Texas had been annexed as well, and two years later California

President James K. Polk was a great believer in Manifest Destiny. His views influenced Britain's decision to agree to the U.S. proposal of ownership of Oregon territory.

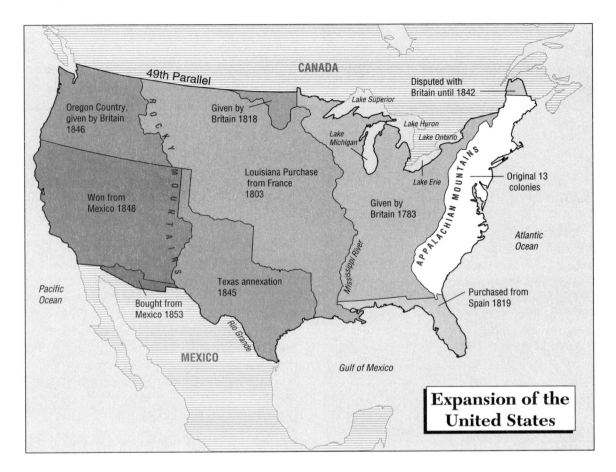

Expansion of the United States

Map labels:
- 49th Parallel
- CANADA
- Oregon Country, given by Britain 1846
- Given by Britain 1818
- Disputed with Britain until 1842
- Lake Superior
- Lake Huron
- Lake Michigan
- Lake Ontario
- Louisiana Purchase from France 1803
- Lake Erie
- Original 13 colonies
- ROCKY MOUNTAINS
- Won from Mexico 1848
- Given by Britain 1783
- APPALACHIAN MOUNTAINS
- Atlantic Ocean
- Pacific Ocean
- Mississippi River
- Texas annexation 1845
- Purchased from Spain 1819
- Bought from Mexico 1853
- Rio Grande
- MEXICO
- Gulf of Mexico

would follow suit. Though Americans did not occupy all of North America, as expansionists like John Sullivan had hoped, they were now firmly settled in from one ocean to the other.

The emigrants had acted as effective agents of Manifest Destiny. A few of them did so deliberately. But most, even if they shared the convictions of the expansionists, would not have crossed the continent and risked their lives for such an abstract goal. The things that motivated them lay closer to their hearts.

1 Why They Went West

In 1851, when Martha Gay was thirteen years old, her father came down with a bad case of what she called "the Western fever."

The Gays had a comfortable home in Springfield, Missouri; Martha's father was making a good living as a cabinetmaker. But, as Gay recorded in her memoirs, he was not content. "He had talked about Oregon and the Columbia River for many years and wanted to go there. He wanted to take his nine sons where they could get land." Then one day

> he received a letter from an old neighbor who had been in Oregon two years. He insisted on father coming West, telling him what a lovely land it was and about the many resources, the genial climate and the rich mines in California.

It was all Martin Gay needed to make up his mind. Ignoring the objections of his wife and younger children, he "at once set about making arrangements for the journey."[3]

By the following April, wrote Gay,

> our home was sold and the household furniture disposed of. . . . Farewell sermons were preached and prayers offered for our safety. . . . Friends and schoolmates were crying all around us. . . . The sad farewells were all spoken. We took a long last look at all, then closed our eyes on the scene and moved forward. Their wails reached us as we moved away. . . .

> The saddest parting of all was when my mother took leave of her aged and sorrowing mother, knowing full well that they would never meet again on earth.[4]

Though being uprooted so suddenly and irrevocably was a wrenching experience for Martha Gay and her family, they had plenty of company in their misery. Farmers and tradesmen throughout the East and the Midwest were dissatisfied with the worn-out land there and were feeling hemmed in by the growing population. For nearly a decade, these discontented folks had been setting out across the Great Plains, hoping to start fresh in the fertile valleys of Oregon.

The Long Journey

When the first few daring souls immigrated to Oregon Country, as it was called in the early 1840s, the vast territory between Missouri and the Pacific Ocean was known to only the Native Americans who lived there and the mountain men who trapped beaver for St. Louis fur companies. Some of these trappers were hired by early emigrants to guide their small wagon trains and pack trains safely across the continent.

But by the time Martha Gay's family went west in 1851, nearly 100,000 settlers and gold seekers had crossed the plains and the Rocky Mountains to Oregon, California, and Utah. Guides were no longer a necessity.

The route was well established and well marked, not only by signs and wagon ruts but by gravestones and bleached bones. Thanks to a popular book by Francis Parkman, even its name was well-known: the Oregon Trail.

The two-thousand-mile trip was a bit less grueling in the 1850s than it had been in the 1840s. Ferries made river crossings safer—and proportionately more expensive. Trading posts and army forts had sprung up to help protect the travelers and supply their needs.

Even so, the journey remained a long and dangerous one, especially for greenhorns, or newcomers unfamiliar with local customs, who had never before encountered deserts or Indians or raging rivers. Why, then, did tens of thousands of emigrants like the Gays dare the dangers and take the Oregon Trail west, creating what writer Julie Fanselow calls "the greatest peacetime migration in the history of the world"?[5]

Historian John D. Unruh Jr. points out that emigrants were influenced by two different kinds of forces. Push factors were those negative elements that made people willing, even eager, to leave "civilization" behind. Pull factors were the positive elements that attracted them specifically to the Far West.

Emigration as Escape

In the mid–nineteenth century the eastern United States was plagued by a number of

The promise of prosperity attracted thousands of settlers to Oregon from among the disaffected populations of the East.

problems serious enough to give a discontented family a nudge strong enough to send them in search of a new life in a new place. One problem was slavery. Historian Huston Horn writes,

> Some abolitionists [those who wanted slavery to be made illegal] found slavery so repugnant . . . that they migrated to fresh territories where they would find no vestiges of the foul practice. Many other people objected to slavery on the simple economic grounds that it put the typical small farmer at an earning disadvantage. A man who owned no slaves just could not raise crops as cheaply and easily as a man who did. Thus he had the choice of going broke or moving on.[6]

Many of the farmers who chose to move on came from Missouri, which, under the terms of the Missouri Compromise, had been admitted to the Union as a slave state in 1821.

The sad state of the economy was another major push factor. According to scholar Lillian Schlissel,

> The real spur to emigration into Oregon was the prolonged depression that swept the country in 1837. By the year's end, banks across the nation had closed, and by 1839 wages fell 30 to 50 percent.

Agricultural prices plummeted. Landowners could not meet mortgage payments. "As farmers surveyed the debacle," writes Schlissel, "they could find fewer and fewer reasons not to escape to better lands."[7]

The emigrants were also hoping to escape disease. In the relatively crowded East, unsanitary conditions allowed typhoid, tuberculosis, scarlet fever, malaria, and yellow fever to flourish. In the 1830s an epidemic of cholera that had been ravaging Europe and Asia was carried to America by infected rats and humans on passenger ships. By 1850 the disease was killing thirty thousand people a year.

Oregon Fever

But the sickness that was more responsible than any other for pushing the settlers westward was purely psychological: "Oregon fever," a new strain of the restlessness that had been infecting Americans for generations.

Some were more susceptible to the fever than others. For many it was chronic. Oregon historian Malcolm Clark Jr. describes these malcontents:

> In their own time they were called not pioneers, but "movers." . . . And they were a special breed, though not in the romantic sense. Restlessness was their dominant trait. The gene of it was passed from father to son.[8]

These "movers" made up a large segment of the emigrants' ranks. Over three-fourths of the families who went west in the mid-1800s had made at least one move before. Many of them had moved repeatedly, sometimes within a very short span of time.

Medorum Crawford remarked of one fellow emigrant and his family:

> They had practically lived in the wagon for more than twenty years, only remaining in one location long enough to make a crop, which they had done in every State and Territory in the Mississippi Valley.[9]

Before transplanting his family to Oregon in 1851, Martin Gay had already moved them from Kentucky to Tennessee to Missouri to Arkansas and back to Missouri again. Lillian Schlissel notes,

Manifest Destiny was spurred by a stream of restless travelers—victims of "Oregon Fever." These people (mostly men) moved their families numerous times in search of a better life.

Most of the emigrants shared certain characteristics. . . . They were children of parents who themselves had moved to new lands. . . . They had owned land before, had cleared land before, and were prepared to clear and own land again. And they were young. Most . . . were between sixteen and thirty-five years of age. [10]

For women, these were the childbearing years. One out of every five females who traveled the trail was pregnant, and nearly every married woman had small children in tow.

At this stage in their lives, most women were primarily interested in stability, in making a good home for their families and raising their children properly. So the decision to uproot the family and take them across the country was nearly always made by a man. Writer Carl N. Degler notes that "the sharpest difference between men and women on the Trail was that the great majority of the women did not want to make the trip in the first place." [11] The man was considered the head of the household, though, so for the most part wives and children felt obliged to abide by his decision.

Once a man was in the grip of Oregon fever, almost nothing would dissuade him. Says Schlissel, "The illness of a family member . . . the advanced age of a parent, a wife's pregnancy, none of these was reason enough to delay." [12]

The allure of free land drew thousands of farmers and young men and women to Oregon.

"The Happy Abode"

If the push factors of dissatisfaction and depression and disease were not enough to make a family sever their ties with the United States, there was the allure of the Oregon Country itself. One of the biggest attractions, especially for a man who, like Martin Gay, had sons wanting to start farms of their own, was the prospect of free land.

In 1842 the U.S. government passed a Preemption Bill that permitted a farmer to "squat" on a piece of property; living there and making improvements gave him first right to purchase the land once it was surveyed. So early settlers with an eye on Oregon assumed that, when the United States got around to annexing Oregon, they would have clear title to land they had "squatted" on. That is, in fact, what happened when Oregon became a territory in 1848.

Not all of Oregon was worth laying claim to. The land east of the Cascade Mountains was dry, desertlike, and considered unfit for agriculture. But the Willamette River Valley in western Oregon was lush and temperate.

In his 1843 travel book, Thomas Farnham assured emigrants that

> few portions of the globe, in my opinion, are to be found so rich in soil, so diversified in surface, or so capable of being rendered the happy abode of an industrious and civilized community. For beauty of scenery and salubrity [healthfulness] of climate, it is not surpassed.[13]

Farnham's description, though certainly enthusiastic, is relatively restrained compared with those given by other early Oregonians who had a vested interest in bringing new settlers to the valley.

Though the British had long been a presence in the Northwest, a considerable number of influential Americans were fiercely determined to see Oregon become part of the United States. One way of making sure that happened was to populate the area with the greatest possible number of fellow Americans. In his 1845 inaugural address, President James K. Polk reinforced this line of thinking:

> Our title to the country of the Oregon is clear and unquestionable and already are our people preparing to perfect that title by occupying it with their wives and children.[14]

Pigs and Elephants

To attract new emigrants, the established ones put a lot of effort into making Oregon sound irresistible and the overland journey sound as simple, short, and safe as possible.

Some accomplished this by writing glowing letters back home, some of which were reprinted in local newspapers. Others trekked east and actively recruited new parties of emigrants, sometimes embellishing the attractions of the area shamelessly.

Peter Burnett, a Missouri lawyer who later became a judge in Oregon's supreme court, told prospective emigrants that the land was a sort of paradise where "the pigs are running about under the great acorn trees, round and fat, and already cooked, with knives and forks sticking in them so that you can cut off a slice whenever you are hungry."[15] We can only hope that Oregon fever had not made his audience so delirious that they failed to recognize a certain element of exaggeration.

Though the more hesitant emigrants needed the assurances of men like Burnett to get them moving, there were plenty of others who required no coaxing at all. They were only too eager to "see the elephant"—that is, to experience something entirely new and different. All that adventuresome souls like these needed was some solid advice on how

Seeing the Elephant

No one is certain how or when the phrase "to see the elephant" originated, but it may have its source in an old joke about a farmer who took his wagon full of produce to town on the same day a circus was there. When the farmer's horse got a look at the circus's resident elephant, the horse bolted, upsetting the wagon and spilling all the vegetables into the road. But the the farmer was unperturbed. "I don't give a hang," he said, "for I have seen the elephant."

One emigrant, quoted in *The West: An Illustrated History*, came upon a party of discouraged fellow travelers who were returning east on the trail. "They had seen the tail of the Elephant," he commented, "and can't bear to look any farther."

to equip themselves for the trail and how best to navigate it.

Early Reports

When the first emigrant trains went west in the early 1840s, there was not much advice available in printed form. The government did its best to help by printing up a report written by John Charles Frémont, an army officer who led an exploring expedition into the Rocky Mountains in 1842. Though Frémont's account was thorough, he had not explored west of the Rockies.

Explorer John Charles Frémont wrote a detailed account of his expedition in the Rocky Mountains. The government printed his work to help westward-bound settlers.

In an attempt to fill the gap, the government drew on another report being written by a naval lieutenant who had explored the mouth of the Columbia River in 1841.

Aside from these two documents, the one thousand or so emigrants who were part of the so-called Great Emigration of 1843 had to rely mainly on information passed on through word of mouth from the few pioneers, such as missionaries Dr. Marcus Whitman and Jason Lee, who had made the trip before.

These accounts sometimes conflicted. Dr. Whitman was confident that a wagon could make it all the way to the coast, even though he had had to cut his own wagon down to a two-wheeled cart and finally abandon it in Idaho. On the other hand, Philip Edwards, another early Oregonian, advised emigrants to send their supplies by ship, because a wagon could not possibly last more than two-thirds of the distance to Oregon. The emigrants proceeded to prove Edwards wrong.

Guidebooks and Moral Support

By 1851, when the Gays set out, a number of guidebooks that covered the route in detail had appeared in print. There was even a map of the trail available at $3 a copy.

Some of the guidebooks were more concerned with luring new settlers to the West than with telling them exactly how to get there. The most shameful example of these self-serving tracts was Lansford Hastings's *The Emigrants' Guide to Oregon and California*. Published in 1845, it recommended a shortcut to California that Hastings himself had never actually traveled. In 1846 the notorious Donner party followed Hastings's route and ended up stranded in the Sierra Nevada for the winter. Thirty-four members of the

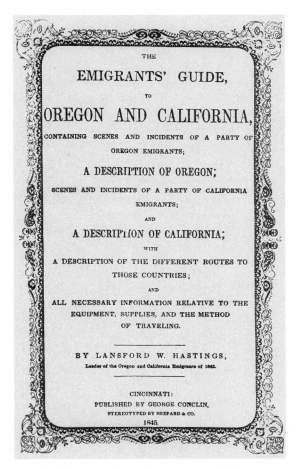

Lansford Hastings's guide recommended an untraveled shortcut to California, the route taken by the doomed Donner party.

party perished, and some of those who survived did so by resorting to cannibalism.

Far luckier were the travelers who set out with copies of more reliable guidebooks, such as those written by Thomas Farnham and Joel Palmer. In a preface to Palmer's 1847 book, *Journal of Travels over the Rocky Mountains*, the publisher boasted:

To the man about to emigrate to Oregon just the kind of information needed is

Prairie Poets

Some emigrants were so delighted to be setting out on what they regarded as a great adventure that they expressed themselves in poetry. J. Goldsborough Bruff jotted in his journal a bit of doggerel that is quoted in *Eye-Witnesses to Wagon Trains West:*

> Hurrah for a trip o'er the plains,
> With wagons and steers and mules;
> No matter for clouds and rains,
> "Go ahead" is the order that rules!

Publishers of guidebooks were not above resorting to verse to appeal to travelers. A stanza on the cover of *The National Wagon Road Guide*, published in 1858 and quoted in *The Pioneers*, read:

> Over the Rocky Mountains' height,
> Like ocean in its tided might,
> The living sea rolls onward, on!
> And onward on, the stream shall pour
> And reach the far Pacific's shore,
> And fill the plains of Oregon.

given. He is informed what is the best season for setting out; the kinds and quantities of necessary outfits; where they may be purchased to the best advantage, so as to save money, time and useless hauling of provisions, and to promote comfort and prevent suffering on the long journey.[16]

Martha Gay recalled in her memoirs, "We had a guide book which informed us of all good camping places. Otherwise, we would have fared much worse."[17]

When it came to actually coping with the hazards of the trail, of course, no guidebook could be of much practical use. "Guidebooks might help them to grass and water," writes author Herbert Eaton, "but once started on the long journey from the Missouri to the Pacific, the emigrants had to rely upon their own good sense, stamina, and courage to see them through."[18]

The books undoubtedly served one very practical function, though. Surely any number of weary women faced with the daunting task of trying to start a cooking fire on the treeless prairie must have succumbed to the temptation to tear a page or two from the guidebook to use as kindling.

Often emigrant families who were too timid to set out on their own found the necessary courage by banding together with other hopefuls in an emigration society.

These societies began forming well before the first wagons actually hit the trail. One of the earliest was the Oregon Provisional Emigration Society of Lynn, Massachusetts, organized in 1838. The group collected dues and published a newspaper. Though it disbanded before an actual wagon train got under way, the society did much to spread information—and misinformation—about the Oregon Country. By 1839 Oregon societies had sprung up in towns throughout Missouri, Illinois, Iowa, Arkansas, and Ohio, infecting thousands more with Oregon fever.

The Path to California

Not all the prospective emigrants had their sights set on Oregon. Enthusiastic reports were being sent east from settlers in California, too. According to one rumor, California was such a healthy spot that an unnamed resident had lived to the ripe old age of 250, and had been forced to move out of the region to die. But when the man's body was returned to California for burial, it was said, the wonderful climate restored him to life.

Though midwesterners were not, by and large, so gullible as to swallow such a tall tale, some were convinced that California was the place to be. Because California was more lawless than Oregon, and less certain of becoming a part of the United States, those who were Oregon bound considered these would-be Californians foolhardy risk takers at best, and immoral and illiterate at worst.

Snobbish emigrants noted that, where the trail split in two, a pile of gold-bearing quartz marked the path to California, while the road to Oregon was indicated by a printed sign. "Those who could read," it was claimed, "took the trail to Oregon."[19]

What They Took

The trail was not the only way of getting to the Pacific Northwest. There was also a sea route. British and American fur traders had been doing business with the local Indians since before the turn of the century, bringing their trade goods not in wagons but in ships.

To go by sea meant a grueling thirteen-thousand-mile, six-month voyage around the tip of South America. For a passenger, the cost was high—about $300 per person. At best the trip was monotonous and unpleasant. The food on board was awful, and sleeping quarters were cramped and smelly. At worst the ship might never reach its destination.

Jason Lee took a troupe of missionaries to Oregon by ship in 1839. Ten years later, after the gold rush began, over 30,000 would take the long trip around Cape Horn to California; 200,000 would take a shorter and more hazardous sea route that included a land crossing of malaria-infested Nicaragua or Panama. But the farming families who made up the bulk of the Oregon Trail traffic simply could not afford the dubious luxury of a sea voyage.

A family who already owned livestock and a wagon might make the overland journey without much of an initial investment. Those who did not have the necessary stock or equipment could expect to pay from $200 to $500 for a decent outfit, depending on the quality and where and when it was purchased.

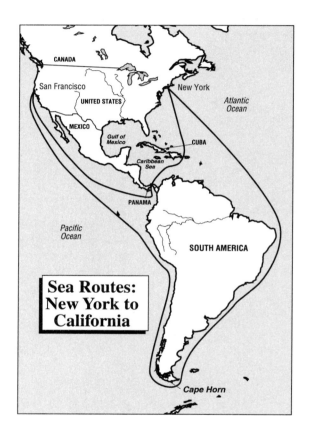

Sea Routes: New York to California

Horses, Mules, or Oxen?

The animals that pulled the wagon were probably the most important element of the outfit and, accordingly, were the biggest single expense. Throughout the entire heyday of the Oregon Trail, a continuing controversy raged, in print and in person, over what draft animals were the best choice for the prairie traveler.

A small minority favored the use of horses, mainly because they were faster than either mules or oxen. But horses had a number of drawbacks. They were expensive to buy—$40 to $50 apiece—and expensive to feed; because horses did not flourish on a strict diet of grass, the owner had to haul a supply of grain. They required a complicated and costly set of harnesses. Horses were also the most likely to be stolen by Indians, who placed a great value on them. For all these reasons, most of the emigrants who did take horses took only one or two for riding purposes, not for pulling wagons.

The heart of the debate, then, concerned the respective merits of mules and oxen. A good mule could fetch as high a price as most horses, and it needed the same sort of harness. And for an Indian, a mule was almost as good a catch as a horse. On the plus side, mules were faster and more surefooted than oxen. They had more endurance than either horses or oxen, and mules could subsist on almost any sort of forage, even cottonwood bark. Their hooves were tough and did not split as easily as those of oxen.

An ox may seem an unlikely choice for a draft animal; it is nothing more than a fully grown bull that has been castrated, like a gelded horse, to make it more docile. Most farmers were accustomed to working with oxen, though, so that made them a natural choice. In addition, oxen were cheaper to buy. A yoke, or pair, normally cost $45 to $55—about half the price of horses or mules. They needed no complicated leather harness, just a wooden yoke. Oxen could also pull heavier loads than mules or horses could.

Even so, it took a minimum of two yoke to handle a wagon carrying six months' worth of supplies—a total weight of nearly a ton. Most guidebooks recommended taking a spare yoke or two of oxen to replace stock that died of thirst, injury, or overwork. Few oxen made it all the way to Oregon—though not for want of trying. Peter Burnett, one of the earliest emigrants, recalled,

> We could see our faithful oxen dying inch by inch, every day becoming weaker. . . . In one or two instances they fell dead under the yoke before they would yield. . . . We found . . . that the ox was the noblest of draft animals upon that trip, and possessed more genuine hardihood and pluck than either mules or horses.[20]

The latter did seem to have a better chance of survival, though. In a letter written home from Oregon, Delazon Smith declared that

Ill-Conceived Plans

Probably every emigrant who crossed the plains wished for some speedier way of making the trip. Several misguided individuals tried to oblige. In 1846 and 1847 an Independence, Missouri, inventor known as Wind-Wagon Thomas experimented with a more literal version of the prairie schooner, a wagon equipped with a mast and sails. Though he claimed his wind-wagon could travel fifteen miles per hour, it had a nasty tendency to crash into the nearest gully.

In 1849 Rufus Porter, founder of *Scientific American* magazine, proposed an even faster means of transportation, which he dubbed the "aerial locomotive"—a one-thousand-foot-long, propeller-driven balloon that could take passengers to California in three days, for the very reasonable fare of $50. Though he had no trouble signing up prospective passengers, he never got around to actually building the airship.

Oxen, the preferred animals for pulling wagons, drink by a stream.

oxen are the very last kind of a team to be preferred! . . . I saw but one dead mule on the entire route! Of the whole number of horses I saw but five dead ones. . . . Whilst of oxen alone I saw, as I should judge, at least 5,000 lying dead by the road side![21]

Of course, one reason the dead oxen so greatly outnumbered the dead horses and mules was that, despite the continuing debate, the majority of the wagons on the trail were pulled by oxen.

Ships for Sailing the Prairie

Little debate existed over what sort of wagon was needed to survive the rigors of the trail.

The huge Conestoga freight wagon used by traders on the relatively undemanding Santa Fe Trail was too large and heavy to haul across mountains and a succession of treacherous rivers, no matter whether mules or oxen were used and no matter how big the team was.

The ideal wagon for westering was designed to be both as light as it reasonably could be and as strong as possible. The wagon bed, or box, was about ten feet long, four feet wide, and two feet deep, and it was constructed of hardwood—usually maple or oak. When the seams between the boards were caulked with tar, a well-built wagon box could float across a river as well as any boat. In fact, the craft were familiarly known as *prairie schooners*, though the term may have arisen from the sail-like appearance of the billowing white canvas tops. Journalist Horace Greeley wrote,

> The white coverings of the many emigrant and transport wagons dotted the landscape, giving the trail the appearance of a river running through great meadows with many ships sailing in its bosom.[22]

The top, or cover, made of closely woven cloth and usually waterproofed with linseed oil, was stretched over five or six bows—U-shaped frames made of hickory. At the front of the cover were flaps that could be tied down; a drawstring or "puckering string" sewn into the other end could be pulled tight to close off the rear opening.

Though the bows left room for a man of average height to stand upright, the interior of the wagon was anything but roomy, especially once all the supplies were loaded. But the pioneers found clever ways to maximize the space. Some built a false floor in the box and divided the space beneath it into storage compartments. Others sewed dozens of pockets of various sizes onto the inside of the cover. Emigrant Catherine Haun recalled, "The pockets of the canvas walls of the wagon held every day needs and toilet articles, as well as small fire arms. The ready shotgun was suspended from the hickory bows."[23]

The wheels, axles, and tongue, collectively known as the running gear, were the crucial elements in the wagon's construction. They took the worst beating and were the most likely parts to need replacing—not an easy task in a country that was mostly treeless. A few emigrants carried spare axles, but most did not want to burden their teams with the extra weight.

Only the tires—the outside rims of the wheels—were iron. In the dry prairie air, the wood of the wheels tended to shrink up, so much so that the tires often fell off. In his guidebook, *The Prairie Traveler*, Captain Randolph B. Marcy advised, "Wheels made of the bois-d'arc, or Osage orangewood, are the best for the plains, as they shrink but little, and seldom want repairing. . . . White oak answers a very good purpose if well seasoned."[24]

On the typical wagon, both the rear and front wheels were large. This made for easier pulling, but poor maneuverability. The front wheels could not turn far in either direction without scraping the wagon box; the tightest

Though inventors tinkered with other forms of travel, the covered wagon served as the main transportation for thousands of emigrants.

turn most wagons could manage was about thirty degrees.

To keep the wheels rolling smoothly, wagon owners regularly packed the hubs with grease or "tar"—usually half tar or resin and half tallow (animal fat)—from a tar bucket that hung from the rear axle. At the front of the wagon was a "jockey box" that served as a storage space for tools and parts, as well as a seat for passengers.

Not every wagon that set out on the trail was alike, of course, any more than every emigrant or group of emigrants was alike. Some drove ordinary farm wagons that had been modified for long-distance travel. Martha Gay wrote,

Many families had started across the plains very poorly prepared for such a journey. Their wagons and teams were

Nineteenth-Century "Bumper Stickers"

The canvas tops of the prairie schooners were not always a uniform white. Some were waterproofed with beeswax, giving a yellow tint to the canvas, others with paint. Often the covers were emblazoned with the owner's name and place of origin or with some slogan. Usually these slogans demonstrated a dogged determination to reach the goal: "Patience and Perseverance," "Oregon or the Grave," "Never Say Die," "Root, Little Hog, or Die." But some displayed political sentiments such as the popular "Oregon—54 40—All or None," a reference to the boundary dispute with Canada. Others expressed nothing more than a quirky sense of humor: "Brest for doze dat spect noting for dey will not be disappointed."

Canvas-covered wagons typically displayed the owner's name, origin, and personal slogan.

Guidebooks observed that too many items loaded into a wagon could make travel unsafe. Many travelers heeded this warning, while others ignored it.

not at all suitable; somewhat light wagons or hacks and small horses for teams. They were dressed in their fine city clothes.[25]

"A Sufficient Supply of Daily Grub"

Others had suitable wagons but insisted on filling them with items of dubious usefulness, despite warnings in guidebooks such as Joel Palmer's that "every thing in the outfit should be as light as the required strength will permit; no useless trumpery should be taken."[26] A. J. McCall scoffed at such overburdened travelers:

> They laid in an over-supply of bacon, flour and beans, and in addition thereto every conceivable jimcrack and useless article that the wildest fancy could devise or human ingenuity could invent—pins and needles, brooms and brushes, ox shoes and horse shoes, lasts and leather, glass beads and hawks-bells, jumping jacks and jews-harps, rings and bracelets, pocket mirrors and pocket-books, calico vests and *boiled shirts*.[27]

Some emigrants, though, went to the other extreme, taking the absolute minimum. Moses Laird recalled that, when he was seventeen,

> I got 2 carpet sacks and packed up my tools, some cloths [clothes], with a large oil cloth coat to protect me from the storms on the plains, and . . . with forty five Dollars in my pocket . . . I shouldered my carpet sacks and started alone from Norwich, Ohio, to try and get through to California or Oregon if I could.[28]

John Hawkins Clark described "a lone pilgrim" who visited him in camp:

> He had taken a notion to visit California and Oregon, and having no money and being impatient of delay had started without it. . . . From camp to camp, from train to train, he borrowed, begged or appropriated a sufficient supply of daily grub to keep him in running trim.[29]

Others who could not afford an outfit of their own attached themselves to some other emigrant or family and were provided with meals and protection in exchange for their labor—plus, perhaps, a small payment of money. A Mr. Cook who had four wagons to cope with had the assistance of "9 men who work & pay him $100, each."[30]

A single traveler such as Moses Laird or the unnamed "lone pilgrim" might set out with no provisions and little money and get by, but an entire family could hardly expect to rely on the kindness of strangers. They could not count on buying supplies along the way or on finding enough wild game to keep them fed, either. The only one of life's necessities they could be reasonably sure of finding was water, and even that was often in short supply. Families basically had to haul with them everything they would need in the way of food, clothing, cooking gear and sewing gear, reading material, and medical supplies for the next six months.

Emigrants who were short on cash might make do with what clothing and household supplies they already had, but most needed to stock up on foods that would travel well, and plenty of them. In his guidebook, Joel Palmer recommended carrying, *for each adult*, a minimum of two hundred pounds of flour, thirty pounds of pilot bread (hardtack), seventy-five pounds of bacon, ten pounds of rice, five pounds of coffee, two pounds of tea, twenty-five pounds of sugar, half a bushel of dried beans, a bushel of dried fruit, two pounds of saleratus (baking soda), ten pounds of salt, and half a bushel of cornmeal.

Packaging was crucial, to keep the food from drawing damp or from spoiling. Sugar could be kept dry in a sack made of rubber (known at the time as "India rubber"). Eggs were packed in cornmeal to protect them and help keep them fresh longer. Bacon was kept edible, more or less, by insulating it in boxes filled with bran. Even so, it would not last for-ever. After just two days on the trail, Alonzo Delano's bacon supply "began to exhibit more signs of life than we had bargained for, having a tendency to walk in insect form."[31]

By the 1850s, desiccated (dried) vegetables were widely available, if a traveler could afford them. So were canned foods, such as peaches, blackberries, or sardines, for those who did not mind hauling the extra weight.

Milk, Medicine, and Money

Many emigrants tied the family milk cow to the rear of the wagon and enjoyed a supply of fresh milk on the trail, sometimes all the way to Oregon. After the morning milking, a covered bucket of milk was hung from the wagon; by evening the jostling of the vehicle had churned the milk into clumps of butter floating in sweet buttermilk.

The wealthier and more ambitious might drive a whole herd of cattle with them, for use as spare draft animals and as a source of fresh meat or to be sold profitably to the

Survival on the journey required hundreds of pounds of flour, pilot bread, bacon, rice, coffee, beans, fruit, salt, and cornmeal.

Although doctors frequently went West to set up their practices, most settlers packed medicine and doctored themselves along the trail.

settlers in Oregon or the Mormon families in Salt Lake City. Generally these "loose herds" proved to be more trouble than they were worth. They traveled more slowly than the wagons, raised clouds of choking dust, strayed or stampeded frequently, and had to be closely guarded to keep Indians from stealing them.

Nearly every large company of emigrants included at least one medical doctor on his way to set up a practice in Oregon or California. However, most of the emigrants were used to doctoring themselves and had brought along a supply of the medicines they were most likely to need: quinine for malaria,

hartshorn for snakebite, laudanum (tincture of opium) as a painkiller, citric acid for scurvy. One woman traveler noted, "A little of the acid mixed with sugar and water and a few drops of essence of lemon made a fine substitute for lemonade."[32]

In addition, wrote pioneer Elizabeth Geer, "Each family should have a bottle of physicking pills [laxatives], a quart of castor oil, a quart of the best rum, and a large vial of peppermint essence [for stomach upsets]."[33]

"I would get my family physician to put up my medicine," advised the Reverend J. L. Yantis, "and if I had a son-in-law who was a physician, I would bring him along if I could."[34]

Even the emigrant who started the journey with all the essential supplies and equipment could not get by without a certain amount of ready cash. Not only was it often necessary to replace a broken wagon part or a dead draft animal, but there were also tolls to be paid.

In the early years of the Oregon Trail, there were already several toll bridges and ferries at major river crossings. Travelers who made the trip from the 1850s on found that what had been the poor man's route to the West had become a commercial highway. Busy ferries such as the one at the Green River crossing charged as much as $7 to take a wagon across, and $1 a head for livestock. Charlotte Pengra, who went over the trail in 1853, suggested that "persons starting this journey should have at least 150 dollars."[35]

No emigrant could possibly be prepared for every eventuality, of course. Still, most were optimistic and confident of making it to Oregon safe and sound. For those who were not so confident, there was the option of buying a life insurance policy. William Gill wrote to his wife that he and his partner "had our lives insured at twenty-five hundred dollars apiece; if we die, you will receive one-half of the insurance money."[36]

Some of the most indispensable items a traveler could take along on the trail were things that money could not buy. In the words of the Reverend Yantis, "I would lay in a good stock of patience and perseverance."[37]

How They Got There

Writers Wallace Stegner and Irene D. Paden have each compared the Oregon Trail to a rope that is raveled at both ends because, although the trail basically followed a single path across most of the Great Plains, it parted into several distinct strands at both the eastern and the western ends.

It is a vivid metaphor, but not exactly an accurate one. Over the two decades or so when the trail saw its heaviest use, the long center section became divided into separate strands, too. That meant travelers who headed west in the later years were faced with a succession of sometimes difficult decisions to make about which route to follow.

In its infancy, the trail was reasonably simple and straightforward. The route it followed was dictated mainly by geography. In their westward movement, American pioneers had always followed rivers, and the Oregon emigrants were no exception.

For a third of its length, the trail ran alongside the broad Platte River, through present-day Nebraska and into Wyoming.

Like the path established by earlier pioneers, the main trail to Oregon ran alongside a riverbank.

Then it followed a tributary of the Platte, the Sweetwater, to South Pass. As far back as 1810, fur traders had discovered that this pass was the easiest, most direct way over the Rocky Mountains.

West of the Rockies the trail wandered a bit, paralleling and crossing a series of smaller streams, until it reached the Snake River. It stuck to the Snake across what is now Idaho, then made a beeline for the Columbia River, which it followed as far as the Dalles. Here, the overland portion of the trail initially ended, and travelers floated down the Columbia to Fort Vancouver.

"A Great Many Curses"

The total length of the journey, from the banks of the Missouri to the banks of the Willamette, was just over two thousand miles.

It was not long before individual emigrants began looking for cutoffs, or shortcuts, that would make the trip less time-consuming, less costly, or less dangerous.

One of the worst stretches was the month-long boat ride down the Columbia River. The fierce rapids claimed the lives of many emigrants; the Indian boatmen charged stiff fees to transport goods and passengers. In 1845, in an attempt to avoid the river route, former fur trapper Stephen Meek guided two hundred emigrant families over an old Indian trail that supposedly led across a pass in the Cascade Mountains to the Willamette River Valley. Lucy Hall Bennett, who was thirteen at the time, recalled:

Part of our train refused to take this cut-off and went by the old immigrant road [along the south bank of the Columbia], but a good many of us followed Meek. . . . The

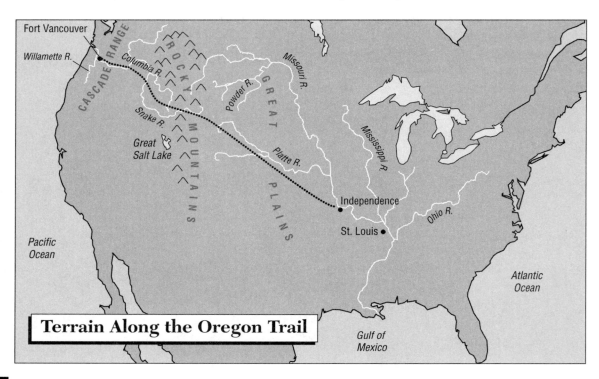

Terrain Along the Oregon Trail

Fort Vancouver
Willamette R.
CASCADE RANGE
Columbia R.
ROCKY MOUNTAINS
Snake R.
Powder R.
Missouri R.
GREAT PLAINS
Great Salt Lake
Platte R.
Mississippi R.
Independence
St. Louis
Ohio R.
Pacific Ocean
Atlantic Ocean
Gulf of Mexico

road we took had been traveled by the Hudson Bay Fur traders, and while it might have been alright for pack horses, it was certainly not adapted to immigrants traveling by ox train. The water was bad, so full of alkali you could hardly drink it. There was little grass and before long our cattle all had sore feet from traveling over the hard sharp rocks. After several of our party died, the men discovered that Meek really knew nothing about the road.[38]

Some of the irate travelers threatened to hang their guide, but several more levelheaded men hid Meek in a wagon. The party turned north toward the Columbia. Meek rode ahead and returned with a rescue party from the Dalles, but some twenty people had already perished from disease, starvation, or drinking water that contained alkali. Another fifty or so later died as a result of the ordeal.

Few of the later emigrants were foolish enough to follow this cutoff, which became known as Meek's Terrible Trail. But a year later Samuel Barlow, an emigrant from Illinois, pioneered a trail that cut across country from the Dalles to Oregon City. To call it a road was stretching a point. Esther Hanna, who traveled it in 1853, wrote,

> I never could have imagined such roads nor could I de'scribe it for it beggars description! Over roots and branches, fallen trees and logs, over streams, through sloughs and marshes, up hill and down— in short, everything that could possibly make it intolerable.[39]

At one point it was so steep that wagon owners had to take their vehicles apart and slide them down the slope or else ease them down with a rope wrapped around a tree trunk. Yet the so-called road did make the boat trip through the treacherous rapids of

"Poisonous unto Death"

Though much of the trail led travelers alongside or across rivers, once the wagons reached the Rockies, sources of water became fewer and farther between.

When a company did come upon a body of water, it was not necessarily drinkable. It might even be deadly, for often it contained alkali—corrosive mineral salts. *The Overland Trail* quotes a passage from John Hawkins Clark's diary that describes

"a desert plain abounding in alkali lakes, poisonous unto death to whatever living thing may partake of their waters. The bones of hundreds of cattle lie strewn here and there over this pestilential district."

If the emigrants were lucky, they might find a warning sign erected by some earlier party. Even so, once the thirsty oxen smelled the water, it was next to impossible to keep the animals from making a mad dash for it and poisoning themselves.

the Columbia unnecessary. It also made Samuel Barlow a small fortune in tolls, at $5 per wagon and 10 cents a head for livestock.

The value of some of the other cutoffs was debatable. The Sublette Cutoff, first traveled in 1844, bypassed a meandering loop of the trail that took emigrants past Fort Bridger in what is now southwest Wyoming. This cutoff became popular during the 1849 California gold rush because it could save eager gold seekers five or six days of traveling time.

But the prospect of saving eighty-five miles or so seemed much less attractive when travelers found that the route led across a bleak, rugged landscape with no shade from

Sublette Cutoff was a fifty-mile "shortcut" on the route to Oregon. Unfortunately, the dry, barren climate and the rough journey made the route hardly worth taking.

the blazing sun, no grass, and no drinkable water. At least the trail was easy to follow; after the first few trains passed through, the way became well marked by abandoned wagons and by the bleached bones and bloated carcasses of animals that had died of thirst or exhaustion on the grueling fifty-mile trek.

To make matters worse, those who took the Sublette Cutoff often did not actually save much time, if any, because the going was so rough. One disgruntled traveler complained that "the cut off was no great affair fix it any way we will. . . . Messrs. Sublette and Co. get a great many curses on all sides."[40]

Certainly Jim Bridger, the famed mountain man, had ample cause to curse the cutoff, for it diverted many prospective customers before they reached his trading post, known as Fort Bridger. At the height of the gold rush, Bridger sent his partner out to camp at South Pass to encourage travelers to take the old route, which was nearly as quick and much safer—and of course just happened to pass by his establishment.

Two Other Trails

Two of the strands that paralleled the main trail for part of the way were not mere cutoffs that veered off the usual route and then merged with it again. They were distinct and separate trails that led to destinations other than Oregon.

One strand was the California Trail. For more than half its length, its route was identical to that of the Oregon Trail. But just west of Soda Springs in what is now eastern Idaho, it struck out to the southwest, headed for the goldfields around Sacramento.

The other strand, called the Mormon Trail, was pioneered by members of the Church of Jesus Christ of Latter Day Saints who were fleeing the religious persecution they had suffered in Ohio, Missouri, and Illinois.

The Mormon Trail's eastern end was at Kanesville, Iowa (later called Council Bluffs). Its western terminus was at Salt Lake City, Utah, founded in 1847 by a group of Mormons led by Brigham Young. Emigrating Mormons followed the Platte River but chose the north bank, mainly to avoid contact with non-Mormon emigrants, whom they called "gentiles."

Back east, Mormons had been killed, burned out, and driven out because of their religious beliefs and their way of life, which in-

cluded the practice of polygamy, or multiple marriages, so naturally they distrusted gentiles.

The northern route was an easier one in that it entailed fewer river crossings, and in later years many non-Mormons opted to follow this strand of the trail as far as the Sweetwater River, where it merged with the original route before breaking off again at Fort Bridger.

Even though three separate ferries crossed the Missouri River at or near Kanesville, the town had more traffic than it could easily handle. Emigrants often had to wait several days before they could get passage on one of the ferries. One large emigrant train occupied an entire week ferrying its seventy wagons to the Nebraska side of the river.

It was not the most desirable place to have to sit out several days or a week. "This Kanesville is a poor little mean place," wrote frustrated traveler Lucy Cooke. Lewis Stout complained, "There is cursing, swearing,

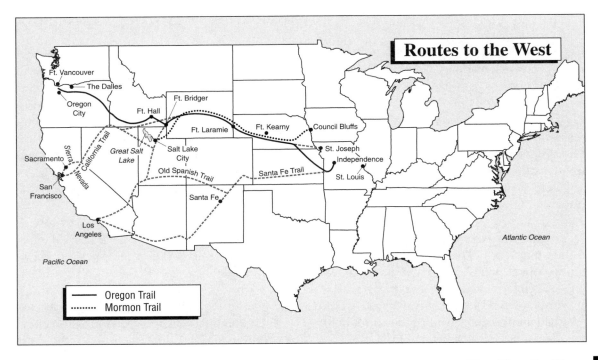

Measuring the Miles

William Clayton, an Englishman who traveled with Brigham Young's pioneering party of Mormons in 1847, was not content to just make a rough estimate of the distance the group had covered each day. In his journal, quoted in *Eye-Witnesses to Wagon Trains West,* Clayton wrote:

"I have counted the revolutions of a wagon wheel to tell the exact distance we have traveled. . . . I measured the circumference of the nigh hind wheel of one of Brother Kimball's wagons. . . . I found the wheel 14 ft 8 inches in circumference, not varying one eighth of an inch. I then calculated how many revolutions it would require for one mile and found it precisely 360."

Within a week Clayton had designed a device that counted the revolutions of the wheel:

"About noon today Brother Appleton Harmon completed the machinery on the wagon called a "roadometer" by adding a wheel to revolve once in ten miles, showing each mile and also each quarter mile we travel, and then casing the whole over so as to secure it from the weather."

blackguarding and everything that tends to indecency going on."[41]

Lucy Cooke's enterprising family at least put their idle time to profitable use:

We gave a concert last night, Ma always having an eye to business. . . . We knew lots of popular songs . . . I played duets with Ma. . . . We borrowed a piano in town, our own team hauling it. Well, after expenses were paid we had $25, so that will pay some ferriages, and it was worth our trouble.[42]

There were a number of other, even busier "jumping-off places" where emigrants could band together in a larger group, buy last-minute supplies for the trail or an entire outfit, and, if necessary, have their wagons and livestock transported across the Missouri River.

Rival Starting Points

The best-known jumping-off place, and the one most often identified with the Oregon Trail, was Independence, Missouri. The town had been established in 1827 as a staging point for another trail, the Santa Fe Trail, and as a supply depot for fur traders.

By the time the earliest Oregon-bound settlers came through in 1832, Independence was still not much to look at. Charles Latrobe described it as "a ragged congeries [collection] of five or six rough-hewn log-huts, two or three clap-board houses, two or three so-called hotels, alias grog-shops [saloons], a few stores."[43]

By 1849, its peak year as a jumping-off point, Independence was a bustling city of about two thousand. The "log-huts" had been replaced by respectable-looking frame houses and business establishments. A sizable number of emigrants had begun their journey in St. Louis and come upriver by steamboat, so when the Missouri shifted its course away from Independence, it took much of the emigrant traffic with it.

St. Joseph, fifty-five miles northwest of Independence, had already attracted emigrants who lived north of the Missouri River. In his guidebook, Joel Palmer noted:

For those emigrating from Ohio, Indiana, Illinois and northern Missouri, Iowa and Michigan, I think St. Joseph the best point; as by taking that route the crossing of several streams (which at the early season we travel are sometimes very high) is avoided.[44]

It also made sense for those traveling by steamboat to continue up the Missouri to St. Joseph before starting overland. By doing so, they could save four days of travel time.

Taking a paddle wheeler upriver to Nebraska City brought travelers even closer to the Platte River. In addition, Nebraska City, unlike Kanesville or St. Joseph, lay on the west bank of the Missouri, saving steamboat passengers the time, trouble, and expense of ferrying their equipment across a major river before they had even gotten started. Unfortunately the landing at Nebraska City was not established until 1854, too late for the nearly forty thousand Oregon-bound emigrants who had already taken the trail.

Several other towns along the Missouri—Fort Leavenworth, Westport, Weston, Plattsmouth—attracted a smaller share of the emigrant traffic.

By the mid-1840s it became obvious that outfitting overlanders was a lucrative busi-

Emigrants often jumped on a boat to travel up the Missouri River, shaving four days off the trip.

ness. Naturally each of the major jumping-off towns did its utmost to steer travelers in its direction by advertising—and often exaggerating—its advantages.

An editorial placed in a local newspaper was one popular method of touting a town. In an 1846 editorial that appeared in the *St. Joseph Gazette* under the heading HO! FOR OREGON AND CALIFORNIA! one writer expressed

Because Independence, Missouri, fell on the trail of thousands of emigrants, it soon became a thriving city and boasted well-built structures, such as this courthouse.

a solicitude in promoting the welfare of those hardy spirits, that are desirous of emigrating there [to Oregon]. I would suggest to them the propriety of selecting *St. Joseph* as the place to which they should all direct their course, possessing as it does, all the facilities for furnishing such necessaries, as may be required for the journey. . . . The route thence is a *direct course* to the South Pass of the Rocky Mountains, and is upwards of ONE HUNDRED MILES nearer than *any other point,* on the western frontier.[45]

Of course, St. Joseph was not a hundred miles nearer than anywhere else along the Missouri River. In fact, the route from Kanesville was about forty miles shorter than the one from St. Joseph.

Overblown claims like these led Captain Marcy to advise in his guidebook,

Information concerning these routes coming from strangers living or owning property near them . . . should be received with great caution and never without corroborating evidence from disinterested sources.[46]

Rival Destinations

Emigrants had to beware of this same sort of biased advice later in the journey as well. Settlements in California regularly sent representatives east along the trail, supposedly with the unselfish aim of helping to guide the emigrants on the last leg of the trip. In actuality at least part of their mission was to attract new settlers to California.

Joel Palmer's party met some persuasive promoters of California at Fort Hall, in eastern Idaho, near where the California Trail branched off. Palmer wrote,

> Great efforts were made to induce the emigrants to pursue the route to California. The most extravagant tales were related respecting the dangers that awaited a trip to Oregon, and of the difficulties and trials to be surmounted. The perils of the way were so magnified as to make us suppose the journey to Oregon almost impossible. . . . On the other hand, as an inducement to pursue the California route, we were informed of the shortness of the route, when compared with that to Oregon; as also of many other superior advantages it possessed.

These "falsehoods," Palmer went on, "so far succeeded as to induce thirty-five or thirty-six wagons to take that trail." But, he added in a footnote, "the emigrants alluded to, not finding California equal . . . to their high wrought anticipations, have made the best of their way to Oregon."[47]

Of course, established residents of Oregon were not above doing all they could to influence travelers, too. Near Fort Laramie, Charles T. Stanton "met a small party from Oregon. . . . On being told that our company was bound for California, they shook their heads, said it was a poor country, but thought Oregon was the Paradise of the world."[48]

Robert C. Keyes, who had gone to California before settling in Oregon, wrote an open letter to the emigrants in 1846, letting them know that Lansford Hastings was on his way "to meet the company from the United States, for the purpose of persuading them from their path and enticing them to California."[49] Keyes warned the travelers not to be taken in by Hastings, for California could not compare with Oregon.

Westbound Meets Eastbound

With so much self-serving advice in circulation, where could emigrants hope to find unbiased information about the trail? Even seasoned guides were known to exaggerate the hazards of the trip to make their services seem indispensable.

Most often the travelers looked to fellow emigrants who had gone before them for a realistic assessment of what lay ahead. Information was passed from emigrant to emigrant in several ways. One was by word of mouth from established settlers who were making a trip east along the trail.

When he met a party of westbound travelers at Fort Hall, Jesse Applegate, an early Oregon settler, complained, "I cannot escape the importunities of the emigrants who are pursuing me into every room of the fort and besieging me with endless questionings on all possible subjects."[50]

Travelers also obtained details about the trail from "go-backs," would-be emigrants who had given up and were returning to their former homes. In 1841, the first year in which an actual wagon train took the trail, about a tenth of the emigrants who had started west turned back at some point. By the late 1840s the annual flow of go-backs numbered in the hundreds.

An 1839 cartoon makes light of the hardships endured by go-backs. Go-backs provided travelers with information of coming hazards and other details about the road ahead.

The emigrants who were headed west pestered these returnees mercilessly for information, to such a degree that the latter deliberately turned off the road when they saw a wagon train approaching.

Still, go-backs did provide many valuable details about distances, about river crossings, about what supplies were available at forts and trading posts, and about the friendly or hostile nature of the Indians the travelers would encounter.

Of course anything the go-backs said had to be taken, as one newspaper editor put it, "with several grains of allowance."[51] After all, emigrants who had met with enough disappointment to make them want to turn back were not likely to paint a very rosy picture of conditions on the trail. Some, in fact, gave such bleak accounts of what lay ahead that

they managed to talk a number of westbound travelers into reconsidering.

Other emigrants profited from the misfortunes of the go-backs by buying up their unneeded draft animals and superfluous supplies. The returnees often served as mail carriers, too, for those who wanted to send letters back east.

"Little Mementoes"

Overlanders also exchanged information via the "roadside telegraph," which consisted of messages posted alongside the trail. The messages were often scrawled on scraps of paper and inserted in the notched end of a stick beside the trail, sometimes with a strip of bright cloth attached as an attention getter.

Those with no paper handy carved their messages into the trunks of trees, painted them on nearby rocks, or penciled them on the smooth, white bones of dead animals—something there was no shortage of on the trail—or even the bones of dead people. "We often saw human skulls bleached by sun and storms lying scattered around," wrote Martha Gay. "After becoming accustomed to seeing so many of them, we would pick them up and read verses which some passerby had written on them, then perhaps add a line or two."[52]

Some locations on the trail—popular campsites, for example, or places where travelers had alternate routes to choose from—accumulated so many messages that they became known as "prairie post offices."

Most of the messages were meant to be helpful. A sign at a water hole near Fort Laramie read, "Look at this—look at this!

The Mail Must Go Through

In the late 1850s the wagon trains began encountering mail wagons rolling by on their monthly trips to and from Fort Laramie, at speeds that the poor plodding emigrants envied.

Soon the mail route extended all the way to California and offered passenger service. In 1860 British explorer Richard Burton traveled by mail coach to Salt Lake City. Though the trip took a mere nineteen days, few could have afforded the fare of $175.

That same year the Pony Express began operations, and for two seasons travelers could thrill to the sight of the express riders galloping past on their mounts and cheer the riders on.

Mail carrying became a popular business in the late 1850s. Here, a rider changes horses to ensure a swift delivery trip across the country.

The water here is poison, and we have lost six of our cattle. Do not let your cattle drink on this bottom."[53] Other signs directed travelers to a good source of water, or denounced some cutoff that had proven not to be worthwhile, or relayed some important news item, such as the death of President Zachary Taylor.

Overland traveler Harriet Ward wrote in 1853, "Oh! what a pleasure to meet with such little mementoes of disinterested benevolence from strangers!"[54]

The roadside telegraph was even known to help the course of true love run more smoothly. John Johnson, a young man who emigrated in 1851, was smitten with a sixteen-year-old girl on the same wagon train, but the two were kept apart by the girl's disapproving father. Johnson and his sweetheart left love notes, signed with a false name, on buffalo skulls along the trail.

Like other sources of information, these roadside signs were not always dependable. "Some of the travellers," wrote overlander J. Goldsborough Bruff, "among other rascalities, are in the habit of putting up erroneous notices to mislead and distress others. I had the pleasure of correcting some of these statements, and thereby prevented misfortune."[55]

The most unreliable method by which emigrants received information was the proverbial grapevine. Most of the rumors dealt with alleged Indian massacres, supposed disasters of various kinds, and reputed shortcuts. Sometimes these bogus reports alarmed emigrants enough to make them seek a safer route unnecessarily. One disgusted emigrant declared, "We cannot rely with any certainty upon the truth of anything we hear as having transpired 5 miles ahead."[56]

4 How a Wagon Train Worked

During the peak years of the California gold rush, an emigrant would have found it practically impossible to travel the trail in isolation. From the end of April, when the grass began to green up on the prairie, until September, when snow started to fall in the Rockies, bringing travel to a halt, an almost unbroken stream of wagons stretched out across the Great Plains.

Near South Pass, reported Franklin Langworthy in 1850, "The road, from morning till night, is crowded like Pearl Street or Broadway."[57]

In 1852, John Kerns noted, "I believe I could count 5,000 wagons this evening in sight." In the same year another man re- ported that "he frequently passed solid processions of wagons three miles long—and often 3 wagons abreast."[58]

Before the gold rush, the trail was not quite so crowded. For safety's sake, most emigrants banded together in large groups. Sometimes these groups were made up of the members of emigrant societies who had agreed to meet at a specific place at a prearranged time. More commonly they were made up of individuals or families who met for the first time at the jumping-off place.

These early emigrants had a lot in common. Most were farmers. Most had come from the Midwest. The biggest share were Missourians, but the neighboring states of

The gold rush brought thousands of settlers West and, at certain times of year, a train of wagons stretched for miles in a continuous, unbroken chain.

Arkansas, Kentucky, and Illinois were well represented. Most were white; some wagon trains deliberately excluded blacks, because they did not want to have to cope with the slavery issue in Oregon Country. Most shared the same destination and the same goal. It might seem natural for them to form into groups for their mutual benefit.

On the other hand, most were fiercely individual and not accustomed to following orders or deciding things by majority rule. They realized, however, that if they were to travel together for nearly two thousand miles, the party had to have some sort of organization and leadership.

Captains and Constitutions

Nearly every train elected a captain early on. Some also chose several officers subordinate in rank to the captain. A few went so far as to draw up a written constitution and bylaws.

Exceptional Emigrants

Not all the travelers on the trail, of course, came from the Midwest, or even from the United States. Lucy Cooke and her family were English. Matthew C. Field was a Scotsman. Jane Gould's company included a German physician.

Not all the emigrants were white, either, despite a law passed by the Oregon legislature that prohibited black settlers. George Washington Bush, a black cattle trader from Missouri, joined a wagon train to Oregon in 1844 and so impressed his fellow emigrants with his generosity and good nature that the legislature passed a bill exempting him from the black-settler laws and granting him a 640-acre homestead.

Pioneer Catherine Haun wrote in her diary,

> After a sufficient number of wagons and people were collected . . . we proceeded to draw up and agree upon a code of general regulations for train government and mutual protection—a necessary precaution when so many were to travel together.[59]

One particularly zealous and law-abiding company even established a court of appeals, an executive branch, and a legislature. But when the remainder of the group realized that these privileged few were exempt from guard duty, they booted the lot of them out of office.

Wagon trains with a single commanding officer tended to function more efficiently, but the burden of duties sometimes grew to be too much for one man to bear. The captain was typically expected to get the train moving each morning, choose a spot for the midday rest, pick a suitable campsite for the evening, schedule guard duty, and oversee the rationing of water and the hunting of game when necessary, not to mention act as an arbiter of disputes between members of the company. William H. Russell, captain of an overland train in 1846, wrote to a friend:

> My duties as commandant are troublesome beyond anything I could conceive of. I am annoyed with all manner of complaints, one will not do this, and another has done something that must be atoned for. . . . I sometimes get out of patience myself, and once I threw up my commission, but to my surprise . . . I was unanimously re-elected. . . . My vanity of course was flattered, and I again after a general lecture resumed the yoke, but how much longer I can consent to serve is very problematical.[60]

To spread the responsibility and the aggravation around, some trains elected a different captain each day. The methods the emigrants used in voting for their favorite candidate could be peculiar. Matthew C. Field described one such display of democracy in action:

> The candidates stood up in a row before the constituents [voters], and at a given signal they wheeled about and marched off, while the general mass *broke* after them "lickity-split", each man forming in behind his favourite, so that every candidate flourished a sort of tail of his own, and the man with the longest tail was elected! . . . "Running for office" is certainly performed in more literal fashion on the prairie than we see the same sort of business performed in town.[61]

If the captain was not an experienced overlander, the company might feel it was necessary to hire a guide, or "pilot." Early trains could usually arrange for a mountain man who was heading west anyway to take them as far as the Rockies. Members of the Great Emigration of 1843 paid $1 each to fur trader John Gantt to guide them to Fort Hall. In 1845 Stephen Meek asked only $250 to pilot a train to Fort Vancouver. Even at that he was overpaid, considering that he led them to disaster.

Even if a group of emigrants set out without a guide initially, they could usually find one somewhere along the trail. By 1850 reliable pilots could be engaged at Fort Kearny, Nebraska, for about $4 a day. Emigrants might even be able to tag along with Jim Bridger on his way to his trading post.

In his guidebook, Captain Marcy recommended using Indians as guides:

Guides were often required to lead large groups of settlers through difficult portions of the trail. Natural barriers, such as the Rocky Mountains, were particularly daunting to travelers.

I know of none who are superior to the Delawares and Shawnee Indians. They have been with me upon several different occasions, and I have invariably found them intelligent, brave, reliable, and in every respect well qualified to fill their positions.[62]

The Need for Speed

One of the main concerns of guides and commanding officers was to make certain the wagon train got over the mountains well before the first snowfall. That meant leaving the jumping-off place as early as possible in the spring.

It did not do to depart too early, though, or the new prairie grass would not have sprouted yet, and the wagon owners would have to haul grain along to feed their animals. Those who used oxen got a later start than those with horses or mules, because cattle are not equipped to graze on short grass.

On the other hand, if it was a busy year for emigration, a company did not dare delay too long or the grass along the dry stretches of the trail would be consumed by livestock on the trains that had set out sooner.

Wagons pulled by slow-moving oxen could not hope to make the two-thousand-mile journey in less than five months. This meant that, in order to reach Oregon before the rainy season began in October, a company had to leave no later than the beginning of May.

It was also crucial to cover as many miles each day as possible, especially on the Great Plains, where travel was relatively easy. On the eastern third of the journey, when the wagons were rolling across the flat bottomland of the Platte, the emigrants could expect to make fifteen or twenty miles a day (a team of mules could cover twenty-five) if there were no major river crossings to slow things down.

Thanks to their large wheels, the wagons could cross a small stream that had a solid bottom without much trouble. Getting a train across a river like the Platte or the Green, however, was a major undertaking that might occupy a day or a week.

At relatively shallow fords, wagon owners sometimes loosened the bolts that fastened the bed to the running gear and placed blocks or poles between the bed and the bolsters, or frame, raising the wagon box six inches or so. If this did not create enough clearance, emigrants might unload all their supplies and lay poles or stretch ropes across the top of the wagon box, then pile the goods on this improvised platform.

When faced with deeper rivers, wagon owners often caulked the seams of the box with tar or covered the box with the waterproof wagon cover and floated it across like a square-prowed boat. Peter Burnett described a similar technique he and his party used:

On July 1st we made three boats by covering our wagon-boxes or beds with green [uncured] buffalo-hides sewed together, stretched tightly over the boxes, flesh side out and tacked on with large tacks.[63]

Anticipating the many river crossings, a few overlanders had deliberately constructed wagons of sheet iron or wood that were more like boats on wheels. Others, when faced with a difficult crossing, took the time and trouble to fashion "bull boats" out of bent willow saplings covered with buffalo hides, or built rafts of various sorts out of several wagon beds, minus the running gear, lashed together.

Once the wagon trains had crossed the plains, the going got even slower. Now the emigrants not only had to contend with crossing rivers, but they had to drag the wagons up steep mountain slopes and lower them down the other side. On the western leg of the journey, travelers considered themselves lucky to make five miles in a day. It was no wonder that so many trains were tempted to take a cutoff that promised to make the journey a few miles shorter.

A Day of Rest?

It was no wonder, either, that even God-fearing emigrants were reluctant to sit idle on a Sunday when they could be moving closer to their destination.

Some trains did observe each Sabbath in the traditional way, by resting. When they reached Oregon with no more than the usual troubles, they were sure that their piety was responsible for their good fortune. In any case, a full day of rest and uninterrupted grazing each week undoubtedly helped keep their draft animals in good shape.

Other trains decided that practical concerns outweighed religious ones. Addison Crane wrote in 1852:

> The question was debated whether we should move on or remain in camp on

Many emigrants used Sundays to rest and let the cattle graze. The majority of people feared losing a day on the trail, however, and put practical considerations above religious observance.

the sabbath, and after considering all of the reasons pro. & con. it was decided that the circumstances in which we were placed justified and required us to travel.

One of the "circumstances" Crane refers to was his company's desire to stay ahead of trains that carried infectious diseases. "Besides the danger of sickness . . . is the further danger and difficulty of having all the grass eaten off ahead of us."[64]

Even when a company did vote to stop for the Sabbath, its members did not necessarily do much resting, as minister's wife Esther Hanna indignantly observed:

> Some want to travel, others want to spend the Sabbath here. . . . They have agreed to stay but might as well be travelling! Some are washing, others fishing and shooting, some sawing and hammering, fixing up their wagons, etc. I had hoped that we would all be a Sabbath-keeping company but such is not the case. They claim that what they do is the work of necessity![65]

Most groups did manage to fit in some sort of Sunday service, though often the minister had to wander about from wagon to wagon in order to find his flock, and even then could not reach them all. On one train, an Oregon-bound missionary "preached to those who would listen, and gave bibles to those who would take them; while at no great distance others were noisily racing horses with Indians of their sort." The service was a great disappointment to one teenage boy on the train, for the missionary prayed to God "to remove the wild beasts and savage men from our pathway."[66] These were the very things the boy had hoped to encounter on the trip.

Eating Dust

Because it was essential to make good time on the trail, most captains got under way at the earliest possible hour and did not call a halt until late in the day. The emigrants were typically routed out of bed at around 4 A.M.—an hour of the morning that most farmers were used to—by the men on guard duty firing their rifles. Wagon train captain William H. Russell described a normal day's schedule:

> We get up at daylight, get breakfast as soon thereafter as practicable, always mean to start or break up the caral [corral, or circle of wagons] at 7 o'clock. At 12 we stop and noon it, rest about an hour, and then travel until between 4 and 5 o'clock P.M.,when we stop for the night.[67]

Each wagon had an assigned position within the train and, ideally, kept it all the way to Oregon. It would not have been fair, of course, for some wagons to always roll along at the head of the train while others always brought up the rear, eating the dust of the lead wagons. So the positions rotated daily; the wagon that had been in the lead the previous day became last in line, the following day it was next to last, and so on, until it worked its way to the front again.

Each family, then, spent much of the trip choking on and blinded by the dust of the wagons ahead of it. On the grassy plains the problem was not usually severe. But in the high plains west of Fort Laramie, it was practically unendurable. The alkali in the dust made the travelers' eyes red, swollen, and itchy, and their lips developed painful cracks. When possible, members of the company walked along several yards to one side of the train, where the dust was not so bad. Some wore goggles to protect their eyes. Those

A refreshing break from the dust and constant jarring motion of the wagons could be found by walking on footpaths that ran parallel to the main trail. Many people did this when riding became unbearable.

with no protection soothed their stinging eyes as best they could with zinc sulfate ointment.

The Foot and Walker Company

Even when the dust level was minimal, many emigrants—unless they were ill or the weather was bad—preferred to join what they called "the Foot and Walker Company" rather than suffer the constant jarring, jolting motion of the wagons, which were seldom equipped with spring suspension. Those who chose to ride did not enjoy it much. Catherine Sager recalled that

> not being accustomed to riding in a covered wagon, the motion made us all sick,

and the uncomfortableness of the situation was increased from the fact that it had set into rain, which made it impossible to roll back the cover and let in the fresh air. It also caused a damp and musty smell that was very nauseating. It took several weeks of travel to overcome this "sea sickness."[68]

By the 1850s the trail had become as wide as forty-five paces (about seventy-five yards) in some spots, as a result of wagons traveling abreast of one another, and emigrants trying to avoid the dust had worn regular footpaths that paralleled the main trail, but at some distance from it. "The paths were nice to walk in," wrote Arabella Clemens, "were free from dust, and usually they led to

How a Wagon Train Worked

all the nice, little shaded nooks along the way."[69] But they could also lead nowhere in particular, as Clemens learned when she followed one trail and wandered about in the dark for hours before she managed to find her way back to the train.

If a wagon was pulled by oxen, the driver had no choice but to walk alongside. Since oxen do not need harnesses or wear bits in their mouths as horses do, they are not guided by reins. Instead, drivers use spoken commands—"gee" for "turn right," "haw" for "turn left"—supplemented by the crack of a whip. Usually the driver was a man, but women sometimes took a turn when the men were out hunting. Lydia Waters wrote, "I . . . learned to drive an ox team on the Platte and my driving was admired by an officer and his wife. . . . I heard them laughing at the thought of a woman driving oxen." Mary Ellen Todd enjoyed cracking the whip and shouting commands; she found "a secret joy in being able to have a power that set things going."[70]

Spending the Night

Around midday the captain customarily called a halt for an hour or two, to give the animals and the human travelers a chance to rest and to eat. There was not usually enough time to cook, so lunches consisted mainly of leftovers, as Addison Crane noted: "Bill of fare Ham raw. Crackers soda, Buckwheat Cakes cold. Melted sugar, Cheese & Water."[71]

Late in the afternoon the guide or the commanding officer scouted ahead for a suitable spot to spend the night. Captain Marcy, being a military man, noted in his guidebook, "One of the most important considerations that should influence the choice of a locality is its capability for defense." Marcy also quoted the advice of an English army doctor: "It is prudent, as now said, in *selecting ground for encampment,* to avoid the immediate vicinity of swamps and rivers. The air is there noxious."[72]

But the emigrants were eager to camp near a stream if possible so that they could water their thirsty stock and have water nearby for cooking and washing. As far as defense, the standard tactic was to corral the wagons. In her diary, Catherine Haun described how this was accomplished:

> When going into camp the "leader wagon" was turned from the road to the right, the next wagon turned to the left, the others following close after and always alternating to right and left. In this way a large circle, or corral, was formed within which the tents were pitched and the oxen herded.[73]

Some of the emigrants did camp in canvas tents as Haun suggests, but it was certainly not the only or even the most common sleeping arrangement. Many found, as Dr. John Dalton did, that in a prairie thunderstorm a tent could be more of a liability than a luxury:

> At nearly the first the wind came whistling & knocked our tent into a *cocked hat.* tearing up the pins and letting the cloth right down upon us, when the rain came through as though there was nothing over us and it required all our exertions to keep the whole concern from blowing away. . . . As soon as the wind slacked a little I . . . went out and repin[n]ed down the tent. . . . I then went to hunt a light and on returning with one, found the boys had all left the tent and crawled into the wagon.[74]

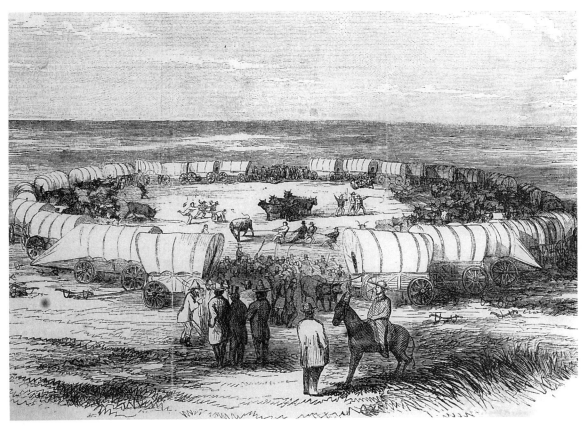

To pitch camp for the night, emigrants arranged their wagons in a circle and herded the cattle into the center. Families placed feather mattresses over their supplies and slept in the wagons or pitched tents nearby.

A childless couple might simply spread feather mattresses over the supplies in the wagon or on ropes stretched across the wagon bed. Members of a larger family often slept under the wagon bed with a canvas or India rubber cloth underneath to keep out the damp.

"Paralyzed with Fear"

The men in the train took turns standing guard at the perimeter of the ring of wagons. According to Jesse Applegate,

All able to bear arms in the party have been formed into three companies, and each of these into four watches. Every third night it is the duty of one of these companies to keep watch and ward over the camp, and it is so arranged that each watch takes its turn of guard duty through the different watches of the night.[75]

In Indian country the sentinels were more nervous. They often fired at shadows. One jumpy guard shot a mule, breaking its neck. Another very nearly killed two women from the train who were out for a stroll.

Occasionally a captain might decide to test the sentinels and the other passengers to see how alert they were. Catherine Haun described what ensued when her train's commanding officer raised a false alarm:

He called: "Indians, Indians!" We were thrown into great confusion and excitement. . . . The women had been instructed to seek shelter in the wagons at such times of danger, but some screamed, others fainted, a few crawled under the wagons and those sleeping in wagons generally followed their husbands out and all of us were nearly paralyzed with fear. Fortunately, we never had occasion to put into actual use this maneuver, but the drill was quite reassuring and certainly we womenfolk would have acted braver had the alarm ever again been sounded.[76]

How They Coped

Though the women on the trains may have quailed at the prospect of fighting off Indians, when faced with the daily challenges of life on the trail, they proved themselves resourceful, hardy, and uncomplaining, even cheerful.

Occasionally they were called upon to drive a team or load and unload wagons, but for the most part they were responsible for the same chores that had long been a woman's lot: cooking, washing dishes and clothing, and watching over the children.

As demanding as these tasks could be on a homestead, they were doubly difficult on the trail. "Oh! horrors," wrote America E. Rollins, "how shall I express it; it is the dreded washing day . . . but washing must be done and procrastination won't do it for me."[77]

Pioneer women were primarily responsible for traditional chores such as washing clothes and watching children, but were sometimes in charge of driving a team or unloading and loading supplies.

The only good opportunity for doing a wash came when the train was camped along a sizable stream. Most women had brought washtubs, but because fuel was scarce, they often had to make do with cold water. The combination of the blazing sun and the harsh lye soap the women used was hard on bare arms. "Camilla and I both burnt our arms very badly while washing," wrote Rebecca Ketcham. "They were red and swollen and painful as though scalded with boiling water." If the train moved on before the clothing had a chance to dry, Jane Kellogg noted, the travelers "wore them just as they dried. We were not particular about our looks."[78]

When the emigrants reached the mountains, there were more opportunities to do a load of wash. Arabella Clemens recalled:

We found so many nice, clear streams of soft water that the men complained about so much washing, saying the women were forever wanting to stop and wash. They argued that, since we traveled in dust, cooked and ate in dust, slept in dust and dirt, and were in it all the time, why should we go to the trouble of washing and cleaning so often?[79]

The Challenge of Cooking

Probably the majority of the families started the journey with a sheet iron cooking stove on board. But once the wagons were on the plains, the stoves became so much dead weight; there was not enough wood to fuel them. Most emigrants soon discarded the heavy stoves along the way and learned how to cook over an open fire, using a cast iron kettle and a spider—an iron skillet with legs long enough to straddle the flames.

Eating utensils were just as basic. Most used tin plates and cups that would not break no matter how they were banged about. There was no room in the typical wagon for a chair or a dining table, so travelers spread out an India rubber sheet as a tablecloth and sat on the ground or on boxes. Because the prairie was so windy, the camp cook often found it necessary to dig a trench and build the fire in it. When one of the frequent thunderstorms rolled in, cooking became even more difficult, if not impossible. Some contented themselves with cold rations. Others rose to the challenge by cooking a meal underground, in a pit filled with hot rocks.

Clothing for Crossing the Country

The voluminous ankle-length dresses that pioneer women usually wore were not well suited to the demands of the trail. Mollie Dorsey Sanford, quoted in *Women's Diaries of the Westward Journey*, recalled that

"it had occurred to me how much easier I could get through the tangled underbrush if I were a man, and I . . . donned an old suit of Father's clothes. . . . It was very funny to all but Mother, who found I am losing all the dignity I ever possessed."

Back east some liberated women had taken to wearing bloomers, a sort of combination skirt and baggy trousers, and they made an appearance on the trail, as well. According to Jane Kellogg, "We wore bloomers all the way, the better to enable us to walk through the sagebrush. They were made with short skirts and pants reaching to the shoe tops."

Most emigrants cooked their food in iron kettles over open fires.

James Clyman described how one intrepid woman "watched and nursed the fire and held an *umbrella* over the fire and her skillet with the greatest composure for near 2 hours and baked enough bread to give us a very plentiful supper!"[80]

Men who were traveling without female companions did not always fare so well. John Hawkins Clark complained:

> We have been eating fried bread ever since leaving the Missouri river and some of the boys are very tired of it. How to bake bread is a question that has often been discussed. Some say on a board before the fire; others tell us a hole in the ground and a fire over it is the way to do it, and still others tell us . . . to bake it in a cast iron Dutch oven.

One of Clark's company found a discarded Dutch oven and "toted it five miles" only to find, when the mud was washed off, that there were two sizable bullet holes in the bottom, and "through those bullet holes vanished all our present hopes of good bread."[81]

Wood of the Cow

Even for those with all the proper cooking utensils, firewood was a continuing problem. The few trees that lined the river valleys were soon cut down and burned. Even trees that served as landmarks on the trail fell to the axes of indiscriminate emigrants. The Lone Pine that once stood in the valley of Oregon's Powder River and the Lone Elm that identified for early travelers one of the first good campsites in Kansas were both gone by 1850.

When the Mormons set up mileage markers along their route, other travelers tore them down and built cooking fires with them. Abandoned wagons and ox yokes were also turned into firewood. John Hawkins Clark wrote, on the western leg of the journey,

> Wild sage covers the whole country, and for what purpose I cannot imagine. . . . A crooked gray stick about four to five feet high, with some branches and a diameter of one to two inches; in the absence of wood we manage to cook with it.[82]

One reliable source of fuel could be found all along the trail in great quantities, provided a traveler was not too squeamish to make use of it: dried cow or buffalo dung, known by the French fur traders as *bois de vache* (wood of the cow) and by the emigrants as "meadow muffins" or "buffalo chips."

Gathering the chips was one job that everyone shared in, according to John Hawkins Clark:

Firewood was scarce along the trail and, in the absence of wood, meat was sometimes cooked over sagebrush or cow manure fires.

"Men, women and children are sometimes seen gathering chips—the men in their arms, the women in their aprons, and the little boys and girls will sometimes be seen carrying them on their heads."[83] The older boys played games with the saucer-shaped chips, seeing who could sail them the farthest.

Some found the notion of cooking their food over animal manure distasteful. "The odor from the new kind of fuel gave our Slap Jacks [pancakes] & broiled meat a strange flavour,"[84] observed one man. But George Donner wrote, "'*Buffalo chips*' are excellent—they kindle quick and retain heat surprisingly. We had this evening Buffalo steaks broiled upon them that had the same flavor they would have had upon hickory coals."[85]

Nathan J. Putnam wryly commented that "it is rather a hard matter that the Buffalo should furnish the meat and then the Fuel to Cook it with but nature seems to have so ordered."[86]

"Hungry All the Time"

Fresh buffalo meat, when it could be found, was a welcome change in the emigrants' mostly monotonous diet. "I relish it well and it agrees with me," wrote Narcissa Whitman. "So long as I have buffalo meat I do not wish anything else."[87]

Charles T. Stanton stated, "I think there is no beef in the world equal to a fine buffalo cow—such a flavor, so rich, so juicy, it makes the mouth water to think of it."[88] A buffalo bull was another matter. According to Richard Hickman, "The meat possessed the most disagreeable odor and taste of anything of the meat kind I have come up with yet."[89]

In any case, Joel Palmer warned that "sometimes eating too freely of fresh buffalo meat causes diarrhoea, and unless it be checked soon prostrates the individual, and leaves him a fit subject for disease."[90]

The early emigrants encountered seemingly endless numbers of buffalo. "I have seen the plains black with them for several days' journey as far as the eye could reach,"[91] wrote John Bidwell, who traveled the trail in 1841.

But as the flow of emigration increased, the buffalo grew scarce. One reason was that the animals grew more wary, as Joel Palmer observed in 1845. "There have been so many companies of emigrants in advance of us, that they have frightened the buffalo from the road."[92]

Another reason was that the buffalo were being killed off at an alarming rate. Isaac Foster was dismayed to find that "the valley of the Platte for 200 miles presents the aspect of the vicinity of a slaughter yard; dotted all over with skeletons of buffaloes; such waste of the creatures that God has made for man seems wicked, but every emigrant seems to wish to signalize himself by killing a buffalo."[93]

By 1852 hunters counted themselves lucky if they came across a single buffalo to shoot. There were other sorts of game, of course, such as pronghorns, which the emigrants called "antelope," ducks, and sage hens. But like the buffalo, their numbers declined as the number of emigrants increased, so later travelers could never be certain of having fresh meat. They had to rely on the limited variety and quantity of the supplies they had brought along. "Emigrants were hungry all the time," recalled Jesse Applegate. "An emigrant not hungry was thought to be ill."[94]

Drinking and Diving

Drinkable water was as hard to come by as decent food. There were clean, clear springs along the trail, such as those at Alcove Springs and Ash Hollow, but the emigrants had no good way of taking large quantities of the water with them. The water barrels that are seen strapped to wagons in Western movies would in reality have added too much weight to the already considerable loads the teams had to pull.

Usually the overlanders drank whatever sort of water was available at rest stops and campsites. The source might be a murky river such as the Platte, a shallow hand-dug well, or even the rainwater that had collected in a buffalo wallow. R. H. P. Snodgrass observed of the sand-laden Platte River, "The water is the color of milk or more yellow and needs to stand and settle before it is fit to use."[95]

Francis Parkman, in his book *The Oregon Trail*, gave an account of a New Englander who dipped a tin cup full of water at a campsite:

"Look here, you," said he; "it's chock-full of animals." The cup, as he held it out, exhibited in fact an extraordinary variety and profusion of animal and vegetable life.[96]

Not surprisingly, the overlanders drank a lot of coffee. It was a good way of disguising the flavor and appearance of the water. As an added benefit, boiling the water for coffee undoubtedly saved a lot of lives by killing off

Because water was scarce and sometimes undrinkable, coffee was used to disguise the flavor. In boiling water for coffee, the settlers also boiled away bacteria and impurities, probably saving many lives.

disease-causing bacteria. One man who came across water so bad that his horse refused to drink it let the animal share his coffee.

Captain Marcy offered several possibilities for purifying water: mixing it with powdered charcoal or alum or the leaves of the prickly pear cactus, filtering it through moss or grass or even just through a handkerchief. Judging from the emigrants' diaries, few took his advice. In any case, though Marcy's methods might have made the water clearer, they would have done nothing to get rid of germs and parasites.

Most of the bathing the travelers did was purely accidental, occurring in the course of crossing a river. But occasionally they found a stream secluded enough to allow a private bath. "Ma and I just have been to bathe in the Sweetwater," wrote Lucy Cooke, "but, oh, it was cold!

We could only take two or three dips and then run out."[97]

A. J. Wigle told of a group of boys who decided to take a dip in the notoriously shallow Platte River:

> The water looked as if it were fifteen or twenty feet deep. Our impetuous Irishman got ready first, took a running start and plunged in head foremost. His head struck the bottom which was only sand and not very solid or it would doubtless have killed him. As it was, he complained of his neck for several days.[98]

"Dor-bugs" and Salamanders

If the discomforts of dust and poor food and water were not enough to make the travelers truly miserable, they could count on the bugs to finish the job. Addison Crane commented:

> I do not wish to be impious—but really it does seem to me that musquitoes, gnats, and sand flies never ought to have been created. . . . They work both day & night, without cessation—a most ungracious and ungentlemanly proceeding.[99]

Father Pierre-Jean de Smet complained of the hordes of mosquitoes, too: "There is no defence against their darts, but to hide under a buffalo skin, or wrap oneself up in some stuff which they cannot pierce, and run the risk of being smothered."[100] Arabella Clemens recalled a night in camp when

> we were suddenly overrun by an army of bugs. I never learned of what species they were, nor whence they came, but in size they were about like beetles. . . . They came swarming into everything. . . . There were bugs everywhere—in our pots and pans, in our tea kettles and coffee pots, in our dishes and water pails, in our food, in our faces, in our hair; yes, in our mouths, if we so much as dared to open them to eat or talk.[101]

These may have been the same pesky insects that Francis Parkman called "dor-bugs."

All in all, the trip was a sorely trying one, and many of those who had anticipated it as an adventure back in April were wondering why by June or July. George L. Curry wrote in 1856 that

> a trip of this kind is the best thing in the world, perhaps, to knock the romance out of a fellow. . . . There are so many little things—trifles, in the main—constantly occurring, of an unpleasant character, that one must call in a good deal of philosophy to his aid not to be entirely disgusted, and driven to take the back track.[102]

An anonymous 1852 overlander eloquently enumerated the many qualities he felt a traveler must have to cope with the westward journey:

> A man must be able to endure heat like a Salamander, mud and water like a muskrat, dust like a toad, and labor like a jackass. He must learn to eat with his unwashed fingers . . . sleep on the ground when it rains, and share his blanket with vermin. . . . He must cease to think, except as to where he may find grass and water and a good camping place.[103]

Privacy on the Plains

In their diaries the emigrants discussed in detail nearly every problem of trail life except one: how they managed to perform basic bodily functions with a modicum of privacy.

Naturally there were no bathroom facilities except at the few forts along the way. On the open plains, there was not even a tree to go behind. Undoubtedly many waited until after dark and strolled away from the camp to relieve themselves. But when there was an Indian scare, no one would have gone far from the protection of the wagons.

During daylight hours, women likely called upon other women to form a shield by spreading out their long skirts. One traveler's letter, quoted in *Overland in 1846,* does mention, "You should have a *Privy* arranged [arranged] in one of the wagons made in the hind part of the wagon," but there is no mention of what sort. Presumably it would be nothing more than a chamber pot that could later be emptied out along the trail—provided its contents did not slosh out first.

CHAPTER 6

How They Interacted with the Indians

Of the myriad problems that plagued travelers on the Oregon Trail, the one that most of them dreaded above all others was an Indian attack. Martha Gay's father, however, was not concerned, or pretended not to be for his family's sake:

> Father told people he was not as much alarmed about the Indians as many other obstacles we might encounter: the swollen streams, the cyclones and dangerous roads, the snow in the mountains, sickness, suffering for water, shortage of fuel and other privations. He thought if we were kind to the Indians they would not molest us.[104]

Though Martin Gay's assessment would turn out to be essentially correct, he could not convince his family of it. They had heard too many tales of Indians butchering settlers and kidnapping their children, and they prepared themselves for the worst:

> The young people were usually all well and ready to defend themselves. We had many talks about how we would manage to escape if the Indians should take us prisoners. We told each other what marks we would leave to guide those who would search for us. We often almost imagined we really were in captivity and then we were frightened.[105]

Relations between emigrants and Indians seem to have gone through three stages.

When the first settlers took the trail in the early 1840s, the Indians they met were mostly tolerant, even friendly, with occasional exceptions.

By the time Martha Gay and her family went west in 1851, the situation had become more uncertain. Most tribes were still not openly hostile, but they had learned to take advantage of the travelers by begging, stealing, and demanding tolls or tributes. From the late 1850s on, the tribes on the western half of the trail became increasingly warlike, and encounters with whites were more often violent.

Of course it is neither possible nor fair to generalize about Indians as a whole, because they were far from being a single, homogeneous culture. Each tribe responded to the emigrants differently, and the attitudes of individual tribe members varied even more, just as the individual emigrants' attitudes toward Indians varied.

A Variety of Tribes

At the eastern end of the trail lived the Kaw, or Kansa—a tribe native to the plains—and the Shawnee and Delaware, transplanted eastern tribes. Francis Parkman, passing through in 1846, noted that the Delaware's numbers were dwindling because they were always fighting— but only with other tribes, not with the emigrants. The Shawnee, he observed, were peaceful and prosperous farmers. Joel Palmer

Nez Percé Indians meet with a white settler. For the most part, the Indians did not fight with settlers, but tribes were often at war with one another.

wrote of the Kaw he encountered, "Although these Indians may be a set of beggarly thieves, they conducted themselves honorably in their dealings with us."[106]

Near Fort Leavenworth, Parkman came upon Kickapoo and Potawatomi villages that consisted of "miniature log-houses, in utter ruin and neglect."[107] Within a few years, some of the Potawatomi would better their situation considerably, by bridging at least three of the local rivers and charging stiff

tolls to cross. "In some ways," writes historian Irene D. Paden, "the pioneers would be relieved to be among Indians who were not quite so civilized."[108]

The Pawnee who lived along the Platte River were mostly peaceful and, Parkman noted, "do not habitually proceed further in their hostility than robbing travellers of their horses and mules."[109] They were, however, continually at war with their neighbors to the west, the Lakota Sioux.

A chief forbids the passage of a wagon train through his territory. With a few exceptions, Indians were mostly friendly and helped travelers on their ride West.

Joel Palmer wrote of the Sioux, "They are a healthy, athletic, good-looking set of men, and have according to the Indian code, a respectable sense of honor, but will steal when they can do so without fear of detection."[110]

On the far side of the Rockies, the emigrants entered the territory of the Shoshone (sometimes called the Snakes). Like the Pawnee, the Shoshone were always warring with the Sioux, as well as with the Crow and Blackfoot tribes, but they had no quarrel with the settlers. In fact, some of the Shoshone women could be friendly to the point of embarrassment. These women had a habit of fix-

ating on some man, not necessarily single, in the wagon trains. If the man returned the woman's affections, she was liable to consider herself his property.

The Shoshone probably offered more aid to the emigrants than any other tribe. Frederick Lander reported to the commissioner of Indian affairs in 1859:

The life of an emigrant was saved by an Indian at "Green River crossing," and great assistance rendered at the same dangerous ford in passing trains, by the mounted warriors of the tribe. Lost stock has been driven in, and, by a paper bearing over nine thousand signatures, the emigrants state "that they have been most kindly treated by the Indians."[111]

Indian children were especially accepting of the emigrants, as Martha Gay recalled:

One pleasant evening some Indian boys wanted to display their skill with bow and arrow. . . . Father got a pan of biscuits and he would measure off a distance, set up one and tell them to shoot at it. The one who struck it first got it for his own. They had considerable sport over the biscuits.[112]

Once in Oregon Country, the travelers encountered the Walla Walla tribe, which

On the Warpath

Occasionally the emigrants got a glimpse of what relations between the various tribes of Indians were like. *The Wake of the Prairie Schooner* recounts an 1852 incident in which Mrs. Francis H. Sawyer's wagon train was overtaken by a party of sixty or so Pawnee who had just engaged in a battle with only thirteen Sioux. Mrs. Sawyer wrote:

"The Sioux had whipped them, killing and scalping two of the party and wounding several others. The Pawnees were very angry and badly frightened. . . . Mr. Sawyer and I drove off the road a short distance to see one of the Indians who had been killed. It was the most horrible sight I ever saw. Four or five arrows were sticking in his body and his scalp was gone, leaving his head bare, bloody and ghastly. I am sorry I went to look at him. I have had the blues ever since."

Joel Palmer characterized as "a greasy, filthy, dirty set of miscreants as ever might be met."[113]

The Cayuse and Nez Percé, by contrast, had "decidedly a better appearance than any I have met; tall and athletic in form, and of great symmetry of person; they are generally well clad, and observe pride in personal cleanliness."[114]

Martha Gay remarked that the Indians in the Willamette Valley—Umatilla and Nez Percé, mostly—"were more civilized and not so war-like as the tribes of the plains and about the Rockies and Snake River."[115] *Civilized*, is, of course, a subjective term; Gay meant that they lived more like whites, in log homes, and spoke English.

Early in the journey Gay had written, "We scarcely ever saw an Indian. Those we did see were very friendly and we hoped we had been mistaken about them as we originally thought they would all want to fight us."[116] By journey's end she had encountered quite a number of Indians of various tribes and found, like most of the emigrants, that they were not the menacing savages she had imagined.

Trouble and Trade

Still, there were negative encounters along the way. Despite the assurances of an Indian agent that his charges were all honest, one of them stole a pair of oxen from the Gay family.

In camp one night the livestock seemed restless, and the company suspected there were Indians about. In the morning they found arrows sticking in the thick hides of several oxen; Martha discovered two more arrows protruding from the canvas of the wagon cover just above her head.

One Sunday a surly-looking Indian came into camp asking for food. Gay recalled,

Native Americans Along the Oregon Trail

One of the men was chewing a piece of ginger root and he gave the savage a bite. The Indian thought to eat it as the white man seemed to do. When it burnt his mouth, he instantly became warlike and drew his gun to shoot the man. He thought he was poisoned. . . . The next morning . . . we saw the same Indian following along near the train. . . . Some of the company wanted to shoot him, but the captain did not approve of such an act.[117]

When two such different cultures came into close contact, misunderstandings like these were bound to occur. Generally both sides made every effort to smooth things over. Sometimes a considerable sacrifice had to be made in the interests of keeping the

peace. Helen H. Clark told of a potentially disastrous incident that took place in 1830 near Fort Kearny:

There was a white man who boasted that he would kill the first Indian he saw, he soon had opportunity of fulfilling his boast as they saw a squaw & he shot her as he would a wild animal & the Indians came on and demanded the fellow to be given up and they had to do it and the Indians skinned him alive.[118]

The emigrants' attitude toward the Indians was no more ambiguous than the feelings the Indians had about the whites. Though they resented the settlers as intruders, they also welcomed the chance to trade with them. In exchange for flour, sugar, coffee, or blankets, or for less useful items such as umbrellas, vests, or hoop skirts, the Plains Indians offered buckskin pants, buffalo meat or robes, and moccasins.

Most were shrewd traders. According to Catherine Haun, "The Indian is a financier of no mean ability and invariably comes out A 1 in a bargain."[119] The experience of one emigrant who sold a rifle to a Shoshone warrior illustrates this. The white man thought he had done well in getting eight gold pieces for the rifle; then he examined the pieces more closely and found they were only worthless tokens from a Cincinnati hardware store.

Jesse Applegate noted that, along the Snake River, the medium of exchange was somewhat different:

Many Indians visited our camp, bringing fish, both fresh and dried, which they exchanged for old clothes, and a number of them strutted around dressed in their newly acquired garments, seeming to enjoy their often absurd appearance as much as we did.

Indians were shrewd traders and often acquired items of great value in exchange for buckskin pants, buffalo meat, robes, and moccasins.

A little farther west, Applegate and his fellow travelers traded with Indians for camas, an edible root, "and found it quite palatable to our keen appetites."[120]

Sometimes the Indians tried to trade for an item the emigrants were not willing to give up. Arabella Clemens recalled how

> one old warrior took a fancy to my red hair, which was braided in two strands and hanging down my back. He wanted to strike up a trade for it, and offered me a pony for my hair. . . . I shook my head, and tried to show him that there was no way of removing my hair. He understood, and unsheathing a great big hunting knife, he made motions to show me that he could cut it off. . . . At this point my sister made a strategic move and offered the old brave a dried apple pie. He took it off to eat it, and being engrossed in the pie, forgot about my hair.[121]

The Sioux were especially taken with red-headed children, and more than one offered to buy not just the hair but the entire child. When the parents refused, the Indian might follow the wagon for days, hoping they would reconsider. Unaware that Indians took such proposals seriously, Martha Gay's father nearly precipitated a crisis:

> Some braves came to our camp one evening to sell ponies. Father asked them in a jesting way how many ponies they would give for Mamie or I. They were at once eager to trade and offered a number of their best. Father then said, "No, I do not want to sell the girls at all." They got angry and we got alarmed and ran and hid in the wagons. Father could not make them understand it was a joke.[122]

Tolls and Tributes

As more and more wagons rolled over the Oregon Trail in the 1850s, the Indians grew less accepting and more alarmed. According to Matthew C. Field, the Indians assumed that every white person in America must be moving west, and some tribes seriously discussed going east to occupy all the land left vacant by the whites.

Many Indians, however, realized that the emigrants were just passing through—for the time being, anyway—and were determined to take advantage of the situation while it lasted by collecting tolls at improved river crossings.

One of the earliest toll bridges, in terms of both the year it was established and its location on the trail, was the one over the Red Vermillion River in Kansas. Louis Vieux, the half-French leader of the Potawatomi tribe, charged travelers $1 per wagon to cross his bridge. During the peak travel season he took in as much as $300 a day. West of St. Joseph, John Hawkins Clark found an even more lucrative toll bridge where

> a large Indian sat at the receipt of customs demanding $1 per wagon for the privilege of crossing over . . . a bridge fifty feet in length, costing perhaps $150. . . . We presented a $5 gold piece but it was refused; he must have "white money with the bird on it," so eight silver half dollars were hunted up and passed over. The Indian was making a "good thing," not less than 1,500 wagons passing over to-day.[123]

At larger river crossings Indians had set up ferries, including one on the Kansas River that, wrote Virgil Pringle in 1846, "consists of two flat boats owned by a Shawnee Indian whose name is Fish."[124]

Communicating Through Charades

In order for the emigrants and Indians to trade, or to be sure of each other's intentions, they had to find some way of communicating. The usual method was through some sort of improvised sign language, kind of like playing charades.

Over time a small repertoire of widely recognized signs grew up, some of which Captain Marcy described in *The Prairie Traveler.* To make the sign for "halt," for example, Marcy said to "raise the right hand with the palm in front, and gradually push it forward and back several times."

Moving the raised hand slowly to the right and left signified "I do not know you. Who are you?" To ask whether strangers were friendly, both hands were raised with the two forefingers locked together. To signal displeasure, one closed hand was placed against the forehead and turned back and forth.

Other tribes collected tolls not for the use of a ferry or bridge but for the use of the grass and wild game that, as the Indians saw it, belonged to them. Sarah Royce described meeting a large group of Indians on the plains:

It turned out that they had gathered to demand the payment of a certain sum per head for every emigrant passing through this part of the country, which they claimed as their own. The men of our company after consultation, resolved that the demand was unreasonable! that the country we were traveling over belonged to the United States, and that these red men had no right to stop us. . . . At the Captain's word of command all the men of the company then armed themselves with every weapon to be found in their wagons.[125]

The Indians reluctantly let the party pass. George L. Curry indignantly recounted a similar encounter:

The advance company of emigrants . . . *were stopped in the road*, on arrival at Laramie, by the Sioux, *and not permitted to pass until tribute had been paid.* The Sioux say they must have tobacco, & c., for the privilege of travelling through their country. Their country, forsooth! Did they not steal it from the Cheyennes, and do they not hold possession of it because they are the more powerful?[126]

Edward Kitchell was much more sympathetic when faced with the Indians' demands:

About a mile back, two Indian Chiefs came up to us with a request that we pay them for the grass our cattle eat. . . . Each waggon then gave something—The Chiefs (Pawnees) spread their buffalo cloaks for the provisions. . . . We apprehend no danger, only from their thieving disposition—They are half starved.[127]

Begging and Stealing

With the buffalo population dwindling, many of the Plains Indians undoubtedly were half starved. Some made no pretense of demanding a toll but asked outright for food. Catherine Haun distastefully observed that "though these prairie redmen were generally friendly they were insistent beggars, often following us for miles and at mealtime disgustingly stood around and solicited food."[128]

Because of the depleted buffalo population, starving Indians went to great lengths to obtain food—including begging and theft.

Captain Marcy wrote in his guidebook,

All the Prairie Indians I have met with are the most inveterate beggars. They will flock around strangers, and, in the most importunate manner, ask for every thing they see, especially tobacco and sugar. . . . The proper way to treat them is to give them at once such articles as are to be disposed of, and then, in a firm and decided manner, let them understand that they are to receive nothing else.[129]

Indians who were truly desperate for food even cut up and ate the decaying carcasses of livestock that had died and been left along the trail by the emigrants.

Many Indian tribes preferred to steal what they wanted, rather than scavenge or beg, and,

in fact, seemed to regard theft, especially of cattle and horses, as a sort of game, with no shame attached. Occasionally, an Indian added insult to injury by selling a horse he had stolen from one train to an overlander on the next train, or by making off with a number of livestock at night and, the following morning, offering to find the "strayed" animals for a fee. Indians pilfered smaller items, too, such as frying pans, money, and handkerchiefs. One emigrant even had his blanket stolen off him as he slept.

In the first two decades of travel on the Oregon Trail, Indians posed little threat to the lives of the emigrants. Certainly they were almost never foolish enough to attack a sizable wagon train, as so many Western novels and films picture them doing, particularly not one that was in a defensive circle. Charles T. Stanton emphasized this in an 1846 letter:

The Indians seldom attack a large body, but only straggling parties of one, two, or three. These they seldom kill unless they resist, but strip them and send them back naked to the camp.[130]

Though the Indians' intent was normally to rob whites, not to kill them, Joel Palmer's guidebook warned:

Persons should always avoid rambling from camp unarmed, or in too small parties; Indians will sometimes seek such opportunities to rob a man of what little effects he has about him; and if he attempts to get away from them with his property, they will sometimes shoot him.[131]

Violent Encounters

Overlanders who died at the hands of Indians represent a small percentage of the total number of emigrants. Historian John D. Unruh estimates that, of the roughly 300,000 travelers who took the Oregon Trail, the California Trail, and the Mormon Trail between 1840 and 1860, only 362 were killed by Indians. During that same time period, an estimated 426 Indians were killed by emigrants.

By 1860, however, relations between Indians and whites were going downhill fast, precipitated in part by the growing presence of the military. Though the army's mission was to protect travelers on the trail, the end result was more bloodshed.

The first major clash between soldiers and Indians took place in August 1854, just east of Fort Laramie. A cow belonging to a Mormon emigrant strayed into a Sioux village, where it was killed by a visitor from another tribe and eaten. At the fort, the emigrant reported the loss, and the army sent out twenty-eight men under the command of a young, inexperienced lieutenant, John Grattan. When the Indians would not turn over the culprit, Grattan fired on them, fatally wounding a chief. In the ensuing battle, which came to be known as "Grattan's Massacre," Grattan and all his men were killed and their bodies mutilated.

The following year, near Ash Hollow, a favorite emigrant campsite in western Nebraska, eighty-six Sioux were killed in a fight with soldiers commanded by General Harney. This battle was called the "Harney Massacre."

After that, hostilities gradually escalated. By 1862 full-scale Indian raids on wagon

Though Indian attacks were rare, the presence of the military escalated tensions between the Indians and the settlers. Military attacks on Indians began a series of raids in which Indians stole from and killed emigrants.

trains had become a reality. Jane Gould recorded in her diary, "We hear many stories of Indians depredations, but do not feel frightened yet." A month later they had more cause for alarm: "We learned that a train of eleven wagons had been plundered of all that was in them and the teams taken and the men killed." [132]

Despite the increased number of violent encounters between whites and Indians, the number of emigrant deaths attributed to Indians remained a relatively small percentage of the total death toll. There were many other, more insidious and unexpected ways in which a traveler could perish on the trail.

CHAPTER 7

How They Came to Grief

As Martin Gay anticipated, it was not the Indians that emigrants had to fear most but the hazards of the trail itself. Accidents of various kinds claimed the lives of dozens of travelers each year, and injured even more.

A distressing number of children were hurt or killed on the journey simply because their parents were too occupied with a multitude of tasks to keep a close eye on their young ones. Nearly every emigrant's diary records at least one instance of a child being run over, usually fatally, by one of the heavy wagons. Nicholas Carriger wrote of how "one boy fell and two wheels run over one leg and the other foot and ancle nearly Cutting the leg off." A week later he noted that one of the company "Cut off the thigh of the boy and he died in the hands of the Operator." [133]

Gilbert L. Cole watched a four-year-old girl tumble from the wagon next to him when her father started up his team. As the wheel rolled across her stomach, Cole saw her "pretty head and hands reaching up on one side of the wheel." [134]

Not all such incidents ended so tragically. Martha Gay told of how "The captain's little two-year-old Tommy fell out of the wagon and before the team could be stopped a wheel had passed over his body and nearly crushed him to death. He suffered terribly for days but finally recovered." [135]

Occasionally a report of this kind actually took on a comic flavor. John Hawkins Clark wrote of meeting an old woman who told him that "one of my grandchildren fell out of the wagon yesterday and both wheels ran plum over his head." As they talked, several young boys began climbing on the cover of the wagon.

The old lady ever on watch called out to "Johnny" to behave himself. "Do you want to fall out again and be killed, Johnny?" "Is that the boy who got run over yesterday? I thought surely he must have been killed." "No, it did not quite kill him, but it made the little rascal holler awfully." [136]

Children who wandered away from the train were liable to become lost. Some, despite frantic searches, were never found. Others, such as Amelia Knight's daughter Lucy, were luckier.

We left unknowingly our Lucy behind, not a soul missed her until we had gone some miles, when we stopped a while to rest the cattle; just then another train drove up behind us with Lucy. She was terribly frightened. . . . She said she was sitting under the bank of the river, when we started, busy watching some wagons cross, and did not know we were ready. [137]

Even children who were kept safely inside the wagons were not necessarily out of harm's way. Lucy Henderson Deady recalled the death of her five-year-old sister:

Tragedies occurred on the open plains because parents were too occupied to keep a careful eye on their children. Children were sometimes left behind, run over by wagons, or lost.

Mother had brought some medicine along. . . . My little sister, Salita Jane wanted to tast it, but I told her she couldn't have it. . . . When Mother tried to awake her later she couldn't arouse her. Lettie had drunk the whole bottle of laudanum. It was too late to save her life.[138]

"Their Lives Pay the Penalty"

Among adults, one of the main causes of accidental death and injury was the careless use of firearms. Most of the farmers had occasionally used rifles for hunting, but now they felt they had to keep guns close at hand for the protection of their families.

Some overdid it considerably. Jacob Snyder spent more on firearms than he spent on his wagon or his food supply. Jessy Thornton reported in 1846 that one party of 130 men carried among them 104 pistols, 155 rifles, and 1,672 pounds of bullets. An observer at Fort Kearny suggested that "arms of all kinds must certainly be scarce in the States, after such a drain as the emigrants must have made upon them."[139]

"Our men are all well armed," wrote Lucy Cooke. "William carries a brace of pistols and a bowie knife. Ain't that blood-curdling? Hope he won't hurt himself."[140]

But many did hurt themselves, or others. In 1841, in the very first train of wagons to head west, a young man ironically named

James Shotwell was killed by a gun that discharged when he was retrieving it from a wagon—muzzle first. This sort of accident was so common that Captain Marcy specifically warned travelers about it in his guidebook:

> These accidents are of frequent occurrence, and the cause is well understood by all, yet men continue to disregard it, and their lives pay the penalty of their indiscretion. It is a wise maxim, which applies with especial force on the prairies, *"Always look to your gun, but never let your gun look at you."* [141]

Lydia Waters's experience with a loaded gun had a more farcical outcome. One of the men in her party had left a cocked shotgun on the wagon seat next to her, and Lydia caught a pocket of her apron or dress on the hammer, setting it off. The buckshot buried itself in the hides of her prized saddle horses, which were tied behind the wagon, and the powder set the wagon cover ablaze. Lydia scooped up handfuls of soggy tea leaves from her teapot and plastered them on the smoldering canvas. Though she blistered her hands badly, she saved the wagon. The horses recovered, too.

Ninety percent of the mishaps involving weapons took place on the eastern half of the journey. By the time the travelers were halfway across the country, they had learned to be more careful with their firearms; they had also grown less fearful of Indian attacks, as Alonzo Delano noted:

> When we first crossed into the Indian territory above St. Joseph, every man displayed his arms in the most approved desperado style, and rarely thought of stirring from the train without his trusty rifle. But no enemies were seen. By degrees the arms were laid aside, and by the time we reached Ft. Laramie all were abandoned except a knife, and sometimes a pistol, which might be seen peeping from a pocket. [142]

"A Watery Grave"

Even more deadly than firearms were river crossings. An estimated total of three hundred emigrants drowned while driving wagons and livestock across a succession of streams that were sometimes swollen with rain. Nearly every account of the journey includes at least one such disaster. In 1853, Celinda Hines stood on the bank of the Sweetwater River and watched helplessly as her father was swept away by the swift current. "An Indian Chief . . . took several of his men who were expert swimmers and divers and made every possible exertion to get the body, but were unsuccessful. . . .Uncle G swam in an got Pa's hat." [143]

At a crossing on the Green River, a wagon with a woman aboard floundered in the water. Though she was screaming frantically, her husband ignored her cries and rescued his team of mules instead. The poor waterlogged woman was saved just in time to prevent her callous husband from being lynched by angry fellow emigrants.

Sometimes the most innocent-looking crossings proved to be the most treacherous. The shallow Platte brought more travelers to grief than any other river, partly because of the uneven, unstable river bed. Lodisia Frizzell wrote of crossing the Platte, "I call this one of the greatest adventures on the whole route, for from the quicksands giving away under the wagon wheels, there is danger of upsetting, which would be a very great disaster indeed." [144]

River crossings accounted for more than three hundred accidental deaths in the westward movement. Wagons sometimes sank or family members were washed into a watery grave by rough river currents.

Many found out just how disastrous. C. A. Kirkpatrick wrote in 1849, "Already within our hearing today twelve men have found a watery grave while crossing with their stock and effects; and yet this makes no impression on the survivors."[145]

In 1852 fourteen Mormon men on horse-back were pushing a herd of cattle across the North Platte when a watchdog on the far bank began barking furiously, frightening the cattle and making them turn back. The horsemen were caught in the middle of the milling herd, and all fourteen drowned.

Bridges and Ferries

As trail traffic increased, permanent ferries were established at many major crossings, making the procedure considerably safer—though not entirely free of risk. Enoch Conyers complained about "those miserable little flatboats, for some accident happens to them nearly every trip they make, and frequently, being so heavily loaded, they sink."[146]

In time, some trouble spots could even be avoided by means of a bridge, such as the one-thousand-foot span of logs that Louis Guinard built in 1858 across the North Platte near Casper, Wyoming.

But many farm families could not afford the tolls at a ferry or a bridge, which usually ranged from $1 to $5 per wagon. In 1850 a particularly greedy entrepreneur was charging $7 per wagon and $1 a head for livestock to cross the Green River on his ferry.

Other travelers were just too impatient to put up with the delay involved. After register-ing with the ferryman, emigrants might have to wait two or three days before their turn came. As she sat idle along the Snake River, Amelia Knight wrote in her diary:

> Our turn to cross will come sometime to-morrow. . . . Our worst trouble at these large rivers is swimming the stock over. Often after swimming half way over the poor things will turn and come out again. At this place, however, there are Indians

Bridges and ferries were the safest ways to cross rivers, but most emigrants had neither the patience nor the money to use them.

who swim the river from morning till night. . . . By paying them a small sum, they will take a horse by the bridle or halter and swim over with him. The rest of the horses all follow and by driving and hurrahing to the cattle they will almost always follow the horses.[147]

Though rivers and firearms and even the wagons themselves could be hazardous to the emigrants' health, the killer they had to fear most was not accident but illness.

Citric Acid and Castor Oil

Infectious disease or some other ailment accounted for nearly nine out of ten emigrant deaths. In addition to the common diseases of the day that afflicted people anywhere—mumps, tuberculosis, smallpox, measles, typhoid—there were several complaints that were brought on by conditions on the trail.

As a result of consuming food and water of questionable quality, nearly every traveler came down sooner or later with the "bloody flux," or dysentery, with its debilitating cramps and diarrhea. When nineteen-year-old Lavinia Porter was suffering from dysentery, an old prospector advised her husband, "What your woman needs is a good, big dose of castor oil [a laxative]. That straightens her out all right." Since she had no castor oil, Lavinia impulsively downed a bottle of hair tonic. To her surprise, "it acted like a charm."[148]

Few victims made such a rapid recovery. Susan Parrish wrote in 1851 that "the bloody flux had so wasted my little sister, Lucy, that we hardly hoped for her life."[149]

On the western half of the trail, both humans and animals suffered from the effects of drinking alkali water. Even eating grass

Disease accounted for nine out of ten deaths among settlers. Grass that had been fed by alkali water could be deadly to cattle, and the water itself posed a risk of illness to both humans and animals.

Cattle and other animals frequently died from consuming alkali water. If caught at an early stage, livestock could be saved by pouring a large dose of grease down the animals' throats.

contaminated with alkali could make livestock ill. Luckily, as Captain Marcy pointed out, "If taken at an early stage, this disease is curable." The treatment involved pouring a large dose of grease down the animal's throat; presumably the grease was meant to coat the stomach lining and protect it from the effects of the alkali. "Many of the emigrants," Marcy added, "have been in the habit of mixing starch or flour in a bucket of water and allowing the animal to drink it."[150]

Another cure recommended by a French trader was to "Take one half-pint each of lard and syrup, warm just sufficiently to mix good, and if the animal is bloated, add to this one-half pint of good vinegar and drench them immediately."[151] The acid in the vinegar would have helped to neutralize the alkali. There is no record of whether the animals' owners tried these cures on themselves.

In the Rocky Mountains the travelers encountered what they called "mountain fever"—either Colorado tick fever or Rocky Mountain spotted fever—but not many died of it. During the last leg of the journey, due to the lack of fresh fruits and vegetables, scurvy could be a problem, but it too was not usually fatal, and it could be treated or prevented by regular doses of citric acid, which many of the emigrants included in their stock of medicines.

Spreading Sickness

The disease that took by far the biggest toll of lives was the one that many overlanders had come west expressly to escape: cholera. No one is certain just how many emigrants the disease actually killed, but judging from contemporary accounts the total was probably in the thousands.

How They Came to Grief **77**

Cholera was no more rampant among the wagon trains than it was back east, but its victims undoubtedly suffered more because they were in such uncomfortable and unfamiliar surroundings, often without any real medical attention.

When the victim was a married man, his wife and children suffered as well. John Clark (not to be confused with John Hawkins Clark) described one such forlorn family:

Passed the grave of an emigrant, just buried, the wife and children still lingering over the new made grave, the company with which they were traveling having moved on. A more desolate looking group than that mother and her five children presented would be hard to find. . . . We stopped to look upon the scene and asked the woman if we could be of any service. "I need nothing," she replied, "but advice— whether I shall pursue my journey or go back to my old home in Illinois." [152]

An epidemic of cholera swept through the eastern United States in the same year that news of the California gold strike did— 1849—and the gold seekers and emigrants, rather than escaping the disease, brought it with them. The unsanitary conditions on the trail helped spread the cholera, but neither the ordinary emigrants nor the doctors who traveled with them were aware of that.

A few made some connection between drinking water and disease. Emigrant Jane D. Kellogg wrote in her diary, "There was an epidemic of cholera all along the Platte River. Think it was caused from drinking water from the holes [shallow wells] dug by campers." [153]

Kellogg was right. Cholera is a waterborne disease. An infected traveler who drank from or washed in a water hole left behind large numbers of *vibrio cholerae*—cholera germs—

that were ingested by the next person to use the water. But the role of bacteria in spreading disease was not yet understood, so the emigrants blamed other elements. "The principal caus of cholera along Platt River is the water," wrote Moses Laird. "The water of Platt River is mixed with alkily." [154]

One mountain man advised putting large quantities of pepper sauce in drinking water. Some guidebooks recommended boiling the water. But, considering the shortage of fuel along the trail, it is doubtful that many followed that advice except when they were boiling water for coffee.

Not Necessarily Cholera

Some of the trail deaths that were chalked up to cholera were probably due to other causes. Emigrant Dr. Anson Henry, quoted in *The Overland Trail*, pointed out that vomiting and diarrhea, two of the symptoms of infectious cholera, were also symptoms of alkali poisoning, dysentery, and so-called cholera morbus, which was brought on by eating too much fresh buffalo meat. In Henry's opinion, many of the victims would have recovered if they had been given a proper diet and been allowed to rest.

"People, however, though sick, would rush on, and the result was death, which was charged to the account of cholera. . . . In cases of cholera morbus, *lay by* until the disease is arrested. If this policy had been rigidly observed on the plains this season, many valuable lives would have been saved, and there would have been a saving of time in the end."

"A Sad Sight"

As it had done in the cities of the east, cholera ravaged the wagon trains headed west. During the peak years of the early 1850s, some large wagon trains lost two-thirds of their number to the disease. Jane Kellogg wrote, "All along the road up the Platte River was a grave yard; most any time of day you could see people burying their dead; some places five or six graves in a row, with board head signs with their names carved on them. It was a sad sight."[155]

The speed with which the disease struck was frightening. A traveler who felt fine rising in the morning might be dead by noon. Usually the victims lingered a bit longer, as Dr. Samuel Ayers noted:

> They are taken with diarrhoea and vomiting, both of which are uncontrollable. . . . After these symptoms have lasted from 12 to 24 hours cramps commence and the patient soon falls into a stage of collapse and dies. Perhaps the average amount of deaths among those who [contract] . . . this disease is one half, which, you know, is very bad.[156]

Some pharmacies offered so-called cholera medicines for sale, but in fact there was no effective treatment. About all that doctors or those nursing the sick could hope to do was ease the pain with morphine or laudanum.

The response of many emigrants to the epidemic was to try to outrun it. Richard Hickman wrote,

> We were in the midst of sickness, pain, and death, and thought if we could manage to out travel the bulk of immigration we would not be so much exposed to the cholera, measles and smallpox, which is scattered along throughout the whole road thus far.[157]

It was not a totally illogical tactic. The cold temperatures found in the high elevations of the Rockies drastically slowed the spread of the disease. Some of the travelers were so panicky that they would not stop to tend properly to their sick but drove on day and night. A number even abandoned victims who were still alive, leaving them for others to bury.

Six Feet Deep

The emigrants were torn between wanting to mark the graves of their dead so the spot would not be lost and wanting to be certain that the grave would not be dug up again by animals. When Ellen Smith's sixteen-year-old daughter was dying, she "told her Mother she wanted . . . a Grave six feet deep for she did nat want the wolves to dig her up and eat her."[158]

In an attempt to prevent this, overlanders buried small children in metal trunks or covered the body with a layer of spiny cactus. Some buried their dead beneath the tracks of the trail itself, so the passing wagons would roll over the spot and erase any trace of it.

The graves needed to be hidden not just from wolves but from Indians who might dig them up to steal the clothing or blankets of the deceased. Sometimes less useful items were stolen: Chief Washakie of the Shoshone proudly wore on his hat a silver coffin plate engraved with the words "Our Baby."

If the disinterred body had been a victim of cholera or smallpox or some other infectious disease, the grave robbers were unknowingly bringing back to their village not just a trophy but a strain of bacteria that would likely wipe out a large percentage of their tribe.

(Top) Graves could be plundered by Indians or animals if they were not well covered. Some settlers resorted to burying their loved ones under the tracks of the trail to prevent detection. (Left) The Mormon Trail gravestone of a cholera victim who died in 1852.

Bringing Out the Bad

Not all the deaths that occurred along the trail were caused by accident or disease, as John Clark recorded:

> In driving across the Mudy Run, or slew where we broke down, the driver of Dunmore's wagon broke the tongue. This

agravated Dunmore so he drew his pistol & shot Dunbar dead. He was tried & hung on our old waggon at sundown.[159]

Godfry Ingrim recounted another case in which a young Missourian, Lafe Tate, intervened in a quarrel between his brother and a man named Miller: "Lafe ran up behind Miller and stuck a knife into his back and as he fell nearly cut his head off." Tate was arrested by a volunteer posse, "but he told the party there was no law on the plains."[160] They proceeded to prove him wrong. A judge and jury and lawyers were chosen; Tate was found guilty and hanged. He was nineteen years old.

These are far from the only examples of murder on the trail. John Hawkins Clark, passing the grave of a murder victim, mused: "How strange that man will commit murder at all, and still stranger when he does it in a desolate country where there is so much need of aid and comfort from one to another."[161]

But in fact it was not so strange. The rigors of the trail had a way of pushing people to the breaking point. "This much I have learned since I started across the continent," wrote Enoch Conyers. "That if there is anything in the world that will bring to the surface a man's bad traits, it is a trip across the continent with an ox team."[162]

What They Found to Enjoy

Though the journey west brought out the bad in some, in others it brought out good qualities. There were many examples of generosity, such as the one Addison Crane recorded in his diary:

> Mr Merriweather (one of our Co.) gave me a sack of flour to day (100 lbs) he having more than he could use—He would take no pay for it—quite generous, as it could have been sold for $12 to $15.[163]

There was cooperation. Emigrants often went out of their way to round up livestock that had strayed and find the rightful owner, or they volunteered to help strangers recover stock stolen by Indians. Others used their teams to pull the wagons of fellow travelers from mud holes.

There was compassion. Despite the threat of cholera, emigrants stopped to assist families who were burying a loved one or to reinter a body that had been dug up by wolves or Indians.

There were even acts of outright heroism, such as the one witnessed by John Hawkins Clark during a crossing of the Platte River:

> I saw one man go down and another would soon have followed had he not been rescued by a negro who, as he heard the cry of "another man drowning," jumped upon a big mule, and then, mule and man, over a steep bank four feet high into the foaming current. Then

came the struggle for life—now on top and then beneath the surface. . . . The mule and his rider and the half drowned man land on a sand bar half a mile below and the excitement of the hour is over.[164]

An Enchanted Land

By the same token, the fact that the emigrants experienced some bad times on the trail did not mean there were not good times, too. For much of the trip, the land around them was new to their eyes and often spectacular. Many of the travelers found the time to appreciate it and remark on it. When he crossed the Rockies, Charles T. Stanton wrote:

> It seems as if I had left the old world behind, and that a new one is dawning upon me. In every step thus far there has been something new, something to attract— Should the remainder of my journey be as interesting, I shall be abundantly repaid for the toils and hardships of this arduous trip.[165]

John Hawkins Clark even waxed eloquent about the troublesome Platte River:

> While looking and viewing this broad sheet of water as it comes rolling down from the great west one almost feels that it has come from fairy land. Picture to yourself a broad river winding through green meadows cov-

ered with grass which grows to the water's edge, beautiful little islands setting like gems upon its bosom, on some bright morning when the sun first spreads his golden rays over the same, and tell me if you do not see "enchanted land." [166]

William Lobenstine, meanwhile, bemoaned his inability to do justice to the scenery around Chimney Rock in western Nebraska:

Had I the talent of a Byron or the skilled hand of a Raphael I might give an adequate idea of the landscape, but as I am, even common language is wanting to give an appropriate description. I thought it, however, romantic, and truly felt more than my tongue may express. O what a pity it is to be deficient of *Brain!* [167]

Nearly every overlander was moved to comment on towering stone landmarks such as Chimney Rock, Courthouse Rock, and Independence Rock, not just because the formations were impressive but also because they represented a series of milestones by which the train could measure its progress.

To mark their passage, many emigrants carved their names in the massive monoliths;

Despite the many hardships and daily toil of the trail, emigrants found joy in the beauty of the scenery and in the company of friends.

those with less time and ambition left their autographs in paint or in some makeshift substitute. James Nesmith told of how he and some other young men

> had the pleasure of waiting on five or six young ladies to pay a visit to Independence Rock. I had the satisfaction of putting the names of Miss Mary Zachary and Miss Jane Mills on the southeast point of the rock, near the road, on a high point. Facing the road, in all the splendor of gunpowder, tar and buffalo grease,

may be seen the name of J. W. Nesmith, from Maine, with an anchor.[168]

After Salt Lake City was settled, the enterprising Mormons often sent one of their number to chisel names and dates into the rock for travelers, for a fee of up to $5.

Cause to Celebrate

Independence Rock, a granite dome that rises from the plains southwest of Casper, Wyoming,

Some overlanders felt that the amazing natural views on parts of the trip actually made the struggle worthwhile.

Most travelers rejoiced when they reached Independence Rock, which was considered a halfway point on the trail to Oregon.

was an especially welcome sight to the weary travelers because it was widely considered the halfway point on the journey to Oregon. In truth, the wagons had covered only a little over eight hundred of the trail's two thousand miles when they reached the rock. Still, it was cause to celebrate. Many reached that point on or near Independence Day, as had the earlier fur trading expeditions that gave the rock its name, so the celebrations were often lavish, or at least as lavish as the remaining supplies would permit. A group that spent the Fourth of July there in 1847 set off homemade fireworks consisting of old wagon hubs packed with gunpowder and blew loose a large chunk of the rock.

Most emigrants observed the Fourth in some fashion, no matter where on the trail they happened to be. James Nesmith's company had gotten only as far as the crossing on the south fork of the Platte, in Nebraska, and spent most of Independence Day fording the river, so festivities were minimal:

> Occasionally you hear something said about mint julips, soda, ice cream, cognac, porter, ale and sherry wine, but the Oregon emigrant must forget these luxuries and, for a time, submit to hard fare, and put up with truly cold-water celebrations, such as we have enjoyed today, namely, drinking cold water, and wading and swimming in it all day.[169]

Enoch Conyers's party, on the other hand, had passed Independence Rock by the Fourth and was camped in "a beautiful little valley" on the Sweetwater River. Their celebration was more elaborate. "A number of wagon beds are being taken to pieces and formed into long tables," wrote Conyers. Some of the ladies fashioned a flag from a white sheet, a red skirt, and a blue jacket. Several of the men brought in a huge snowball impaled on a pole. "The snowball was brought into use making a fine lot of Sweetwater Mountain ice cream." Also on the menu were roast antelope, sage hen, and rabbit, baked beans, warm rolls, and a surprising variety of pies and cakes. "No person left the table hungry. After our feast patriotic songs were indulged in, winding up with three cheers for Uncle Sam and three for Old Glory." [170]

Soda, Beer, and Steamboats

Several other natural features along the trail awed almost all the emigrants who saw them. Saleratus Lake, along the Sweetwater River, appeared at first to be just another alkali lake, "a mud hole of some four or five acres across," as John Hawkins Clark described it. But around it was "a crust of four or five inches of crude saleratus [bicarbonate of soda] of a yellowish color." [171]

Like many of the emigrants, Nathan Putnam put the deposits of soda to good use: "We have procured a bucket full and use it evry day in makeing our bread I like it much better than the salaratus which you get in the Grocerys." [172]

Soda Springs, in eastern Idaho, proved similarly useful, according to Esther Hanna:

> The water is clear and sparkling, boiling and bubbling, swelling at times almost to the surface. It is strongly impregnated with soda, and by putting a little acid in it and adding sugar, it makes an excellent drink. It will compare with any soda as it foams and boils up in the same way. It will also raise biscuit equal to saleratus. [173]

South Pass and Icy Slough

Overlanders found that few things about the journey were quite the way they had expected. One of the biggest surprises was South Pass. Its summit was such an important milestone, marking as it did both the halfway point of the trail and the Continental Divide, that most expected something rather dramatic.

But when they reached it, instead of a steep, narrow passage with mountains rising sharply on either side, travelers found a broad, gradual slope that looked more like a meadow than a mountain pass.

According to the diary of John Hawkins Clark, quoted in *The Overland Trail*, "The Pass is quite level; so much so that it is hard for the traveler to locate the exact spot he can call the summit." Many were not aware that they had crossed the divide until they noticed that the streams they came across were flowing west, not east.

The area around South Pass did have one extraordinary feature—a spot called Ice Slough, or Icy Slough. The slough was a bed of solid ice that lay a foot below the surface of the ground. Some of the astonished emigrants dug the dirt away and chipped off chunks of ice to chill their drinking water.

Not everyone agreed about the water's drinkability. One skeptical man remarked, "These women are strange beings, and would drink anything that is called fashionable." [174]

A little farther along, the travelers came upon Beer Spring. "Its water," noted Lydia Waters, "looked exactly like Lager Beer, and tasted as if it were, only flat." [175] Reputedly, if a person drank very much of it, it even produced "a kind of giddiness like intoxication."[176]

Nearby Steamboat Spring spouted gas that, according to Joel Palmer, "produces a sound similar to the puffing of a steamboat, but not so deep. It can frequently be heard at the distance of a quarter of a mile."[177] Young boys from the wagon trains delighted in plugging the exit hole with sod or grass and watching the gas blow the blockage skyward. When one boy clamped his hat over the hole, the pressure blew off the top of the hat.

Palmer also found in Idaho a group of springs that were hot enough to cook food—and the nose of a curious ox that tried to drink the water.

"The Fair Oregon Girls!"

Another feature of life on the trail that appealed to many emigrants, especially those used to a solitary existence on a farm, was the companionship to be found on the wagon train. Catherine Haun wrote,

> During the day we womenfolk visited from wagon to wagon or congenial friends spent an hour walking, ever westward, and talking over our home life back in "the states" telling of the loved ones left behind; voicing our hopes for the future in the far west and even whispering a little friendly gossip of emigrant life.[178]

For young, unmarried men and women, the trip offered a chance to make new acquaintances of the opposite sex, and romance often blossomed. The young men in Charles Stanton's company were heartbroken when twenty of the wagons split off into a separate train:

In their party there were many young ladies—in ours, mostly young men. Friendships and attachments had been formed which were hard to break; for, ever since, our company is nearly deserted, by the young men every day riding out on horseback, pretending to hunt, but instead of pursuing the bounding deer or fleet antelope, they are generally found among the fair Oregon girls![179]

When a wagon train romance led to a wedding, another celebration, known as a "chivaree," was in order. Rebecca Woodson described the wedding night of a friend:

> The newly married couple occupied a wagon for sleeping apartments. The first notice they had of any disturbance was when most of the men and women in the company took hold . . . and ran the wagon a half mile out on the prairie. Then the fun began. Such banging of cans shooting of guns, etc. and every noice conceivable was resorted to. The disturbance was kept up until midnight.[180]

The birth of a child, when it went well, was another happy occasion, and one that happened fairly frequently. One small company that went west in 1847 saw the birth of five babies along the way.

Accordians and Conundrums

The emigrants did not need a specific occasion as an excuse to have a good time. When the day's travel had been relatively easy, the travelers had the time and energy after supper was over to relax and enjoy themselves a bit. "We spent many happy hours with our neighbors in camp," recalled Martha Gay,

An emigrant dances at a wagon train encampment. Musicians frequently accompanied travelers and dancing was a favorite pastime of many settlers.

"talking and singing, telling stories, guessing conundrums [riddles]."[181]

Sometimes they engaged in more organized activities. Jane Gould wrote in her diary, "The men had a ball-play towards night. Seemed to enjoy themselves very much, it seemed like old times."[182]

Music was another favorite pastime. Nearly every company included one or more amateur musicians. Enoch Conyers came across a party of "four richly dressed young ladies and two young girls. . . . One of the young ladies was making music on an accordean, another was playing on a guitar."[183]

Music often led to dancing. Jesse Applegate described such a night in camp:

Before a tent near the river a violin makes lively music, and some youths and maidens have improvised a dance upon the green; in another quarter a flute gives its mellow and melancholy notes to the still air, which as they float away over the quiet river seem a lament for the past rather than hope for the future.[184]

When there were not enough women in the train to provide dancing partners for all, a number of the men might be drafted to fill the roles; handkerchiefs tied around their heads identified them as "ladies."

Five Forts

One of the few things on the trail the emigrants could really look forward to was arriving at a fort or trading post. By the late 1840s there were five such establishments along the way, at widely spaced intervals. Though most were not much to look at, they at least offered some semblance of civilization.

Fort Kearny, on the Platte River in central Nebraska, was established in 1848 specifically to protect travelers on the trail. It consisted of several sod huts, one store, one smithy, and a few soldiers who would have rather been anywhere else. But emigrants could mail letters here and purchase supplies.

When travelers reached Fort Laramie in present-day Wyoming, it meant they were roughly one-third of the way to their destination. An emigrant writing in 1852 was impressed with the fort:

There were five major, widely spaced forts along the Oregon Trail. Fort Laramie represented one-third of the distance to Oregon.

I find the buildings in good repair . . . the dwellings are of frame, two stories high with double porches and railings, painted white; the small outbuildings, stables, & c., are of *adobes*. There is a good blacksmith and wagon maker's shop here . . . there are also three bakeries, where the poor emigrant can obtain an apology for a loaf of bread for 40 cents, and a small dried apple pie for 50 cents.[185]

Other prices were high at the fort, too: Sugar was 75 cents a pound, tea $2 a pound. But a lucky traveler might find a bargain. Robert Laws paid only 25 cents for a pint of buttermilk with ice in it, a loaf of bread, and a piece of roasted buffalo meat; "this was," he wrote, "the best meal I ever eat."[186] It must have seemed so, after the monotonous diet on the trail.

Challenging the Columbia

Before the Barlow road opened in 1846, a number of emigrants met with disaster on the Columbia River—not in crossing it but in floating down it to the mouth of the Willamette, a trip that could take as much as a month.

Those who could afford it hired Indian boatmen to transport them and their supplies downriver. Those who had little money left built boats of their own. Most were sorry they had when they saw the raging rapids they had to navigate. Jesse Applegate's party took two hastily constructed boats down the Columbia in 1843. One of the craft survived. The other was swept under in a whirlpool, drowning nine-year-olds Warren and Edward Applegate as well as an old emigrant who tried to rescue Edward.

From 1858 on, Fort Bridger in southwest Wyoming was an army outpost, but in the early days of the trail it was just a trading post, and not a very appealing one. Joel Palmer wrote in his guidebook, "It is built of poles and daubed with mud; it is a shabby concern."[187]

But the area around it did provide sweet water and good grazing, and Bridger's store offered powder and lead, tobacco and whiskey, as well as clothing, including buckskin suits that sold for $25. Bridger also sold, for $40 a yoke, "recruited" oxen—that is, oxen that he had bought cheaply from other emigrants and that were now rested and fattened up.

Like Fort Bridger, Fort Hall in Idaho was originally a fur trading post. Though it was owned by the Hudson's Bay Company after 1837, emigrants could purchase supplies here and often question established settlers from Oregon and California about what lay ahead. Sometimes the information they got was even accurate.

Fort Boise was the last stop before Oregon Country. By this point many emigrants were running dangerously low on supplies and, if they had any money left, they were likely to wipe out the fort's stock of flour, tea, coffee, and other staples.

Unless they took a detour to Fort Walla Walla or floated down the Columbia to Fort Vancouver, also owned by the Hudson's Bay Company, the overlanders were on their own now until they reached Oregon City, on the Willamette River.

A Discontented Community

For most of the emigrants, the high point of the journey was getting to the end of it. "We rejoiced to know that we had at last arrived in Oregon settlements after five long months,"[188] wrote Martha Gay.

Opinions of Oregon varied, ranging from contentment to bitter hatred. Once they had reached their destination, a few restless settlers found themselves back on the trail.

But the fact that they had reached their destination at long last did not mean the pioneers could now just sit back and relax and recuperate from the ordeal. There were houses to be built and crops to be planted. "A lazy person should never think of going to Oregon,"[189] commented Elizabeth Wood.

The new settlers' reactions to the new land varied as much as their individual personalities did. Nathaniel Ford was well satisfied:

We had a tedious and tiring trip; but I think we are well paid for our trouble; we are in the best country I have ever seen for farming and stock raising. . . . My family are healthier than they ever were before.[190]

At the opposite end of the spectrum was Hezekiah Packingham's sour assessment: "I arrived in the Wallamette Valley on the 30th of September, and my calculations are all defeated about Oregon. I found it a mean, dried up, and drowned country."[191]

Inevitably, there were those who could not be content in Oregon no matter how appealing they found it. The restlessness that

The Helpful Hudson's Bay Company

Many of the new settlers in the Northwest, resentful of the British presence there, tried to put the Hudson's Bay Company in a bad light by accusing its employees of steering emigrants away from Oregon, which the British hoped to claim, and toward California.

These accusations were probably unfair and unfounded. There is no question that the company was dismayed by the influx of Americans, and it was the official policy to discourage the emigrants. But Dr. John McLoughlin, the man in charge of the company's trading post at Fort Vancouver, ignored official policy. He and his men repeatedly went out of their way to aid the emigrants, providing them with food, shelter, tools and seed, medical attention, and even passage down the Columbia in company boats.

had driven the "movers" to the Far West in the first place did not simply disappear once they got there. James Clyman, who arrived in Oregon Country in 1844, wrote to a friend back east:

I never saw a more discontented community, owing principally to natural disposition. Nearly all, like myself, having been of a roving discontented character before leaving their eastern homes. The long tiresome trip from the States, has taught them what they are capable of performing and enduring. They talk of removing to the Islands [Hawaii], California, Chili, and other parts of South America with as much composure as you in Wisconsin talk of removing to Indiana or Michigan.[192]

Many of the overlanders who had suffered from Oregon fever now found themselves with a case of gold fever, and they moved on to California. Even Martha Gay's father, who for years had dreamed of making a home in the Willamette Valley, could not seem to settle in there. He moved the family yet again, to southern Oregon, where things were less civilized. "We did not like the place very well," commented Martha. "We had come West to live in the Willamette Valley and we were not ready to leave it and live so isolated."[193]

The End of the Trail

Around 1855 the epidemic of Oregon fever began to die down, as more and more settlers discovered that they did not need to go so far west to find fertile, uncrowded land.

For many years the Great Plains had been considered a vast wasteland—the Great American Desert, some called it. Explorer Stephen H. Long pronounced it "unfit for cultivation and, of course, uninhabitable by a people depending upon agriculture for their subsistence."[194]

But the overlanders had found that this was not an accurate picture of the plains. Instead, Addison Crane noted, "Every acre as far as the eye could see was clothed with verdure [green vegetation], and the soil is as the best of Indiana."[195]

As reports like these made their way east, more and more discontented farmers thought of relocating to the Great Plains. The influx of settlers increased with the passage of the Kansas-Nebraska Act of 1854, which officially opened up Indian territory to white land seekers, and the Homestead Act of 1862, which allowed any citizen or alien immigrant to claim 160 acres of land simply by living on it and farming it for five years.

Some emigrants, such as Arabella Clemens and her family, still went to the Far West in the 1860s to escape the ravages of the Civil War. In the years just after the war, travel on the plains became increasingly dangerous as the Sioux and the Cheyenne tried to exclude whites from their land, and bands of outlaws preyed on travelers. Still, some twenty-five thousand new emigrants made the overland journey in the postwar period. It was the final chapter in the saga of the wagon trains.

In 1869 the Central and Union Pacific Railroad completed construction on a line from Omaha to Sacramento, turning a grueling trip that had required five or six months and an immense amount of fortitude into one that could be accomplished in less than a week, and in relative ease and comfort.

Traces of Their Passage

But the Oregon Trail did not vanish completely. So many wagons had traveled over it during its heyday that traces of their passage can still be seen today.

Wagon ruts are visible at various sites across the country, including Rock Creek Station State Park in southeastern Nebraska, California Hill just west of Brule, Nebraska, and Bonneville Point, just off Interstate 84 southeast of Boise, Idaho.

Near Guernsey, Wyoming, ruts nearly five feet deep are worn into the soft sandstone at Oregon Trail Ruts State Historic Site. Nearby is Register Cliff, where a sharp eye can still make out names carved in the rock by emigrants a century and a half ago. Travelers' signatures are also still visible atop Independence Rock, about fifty miles southeast of Casper, Wyoming, on Highway 220.

There are dozens of other historic sites along the route of the trail, including restored forts at Fort Kearny State Historical Park in

The construction of the Central and Union Pacific Railroad. The railroad provided emigrants with a quick and comfortable trip west, rendering wagon trains obsolete.

Nebraska, Fort Laramie National Historic Site in Wyoming, Fort Hall near Pocatello, Idaho, and Fort Boise in Parma, Idaho.

Several museums give an overview of the trail's history: the Museum of Westward Expansion, located beneath the Gateway Arch in St. Louis; the National Frontier Trails Center in Independence, Missouri; and the End of the Oregon Trail Interpretive Center in Oregon City, Oregon.

Notes

Introduction: Agents of Manifest Destiny

1. Quoted in Editors of Time-Life Books, *The Trailblazers*. New York: Time-Life, 1973, p. 158.
2. Quoted in Editors of Time-Life Books, *The Pioneers*. New York: Time-Life, 1974, p. 43.

Chapter 1: Why They Went West

3. Martha Gay Masterson, *One Woman's West: Recollections of the Oregon Trail and Settling the Northwest Country*, ed. Lois Barton, Eugene, OR: Spencer Butte Press, 1986, p. 23.
4. Masterson, *One Woman's West*, pp. 26–28.
5. Julie Fanselow, *The Traveler's Guide to the Oregon Trail*. Helena, MT: Falcon Press, 1992, p. 4.
6. Quoted in Editors of Time-Life Books, *The Pioneers*, p. 25.
7. Lillian Schlissel, *Women's Diaries of the Westward Journey*. New York: Schocken, 1982, pp. 19–20.
8. Malcolm Clark Jr., *Eden Seekers: The Settlement of Oregon, 1818–1862*. Boston: Houghton Mifflin, 1981, p. 5.
9. Quoted in John D. Unruh Jr., *The Plains Across: The Overland Emigrants and the Trans-Mississippi West, 1840–60*. Urbana: University of Illinois Press, 1979, pp. 90–91.
10. Schlissel, *Women's Diaries*, pp. 27–28.
11. Quoted in Schlissel, *Women's Diaries*, p. 6.
12. Schlissel, *Women's Diaries*, p. 30.
13. Thomas J. Farnham, *Travels in the Great Western Prairies, the Anahuac and Rocky Mountains, and in the Oregon Territory*. New York: Da Capo Press, 1973, p. 315.
14. Quoted in Fanselow, *The Traveler's Guide*, p. 19.
15. Quoted in Editors of Time-Life Books, *The Pioneers*, p. 19.
16. Joel Palmer, *Journal of Travels over the Rocky Mountains*. Ann Arbor, MI: University Microfilms, 1966, p. v.
17. Masterson, *One Woman's West*, p. 38
18. Herbert Eaton, *The Overland Trail to California in 1852*. New York: Putnam's, 1974, p. 2.
19. Quoted in Unruh, *The Plains Across*, p. 93.

Chapter 2: What They Took

20. Quoted in James Hewitt, ed., *Eye-Witnesses to Wagon Trains West*. New York: Scribner's, 1973, p. 48.
21. Quoted in Eaton, *The Overland Trail*, pp. 4–5.
22. Quoted in Irene D. Paden, *The Wake of the Prairie Schooner*. New York: Macmillan, 1947, p. 63.
23. Quoted in Schlissel, *Women's Diaries*, p. 168.
24. Randolph B. Marcy, *The Prairie Traveler: A Hand-Book for Overland Expeditions*. Williamstown, MA: Corner House, 1968, p. 26
25. Masterson, *One Woman's West*, p. 45.
26. Palmer, *Journal of Travels*, p. 142.
27. Quoted in Editors of Time-Life Books, *The Pioneers*, p. 88.
28. Quoted in Eaton, *The Overland Trail*, p. 14.

29. Quoted in Eaton, *The Overland Trail,* p. 198.
30. Quoted in Eaton, *The Overland Trail,* pp. 186–87.
31. Quoted in Editors of Time-Life Books, *The Pioneers,* p. 88.
32. Quoted in Schlissel, *Women's Diaries,* p. 60.
33. Quoted in Schlissel, *Women's Diaries,* p. 60.
34. Quoted in Eaton, *The Overland Trail,* p. 10.
35. Quoted in Schlissel, *Women's Diaries,* p. 77.
36. Quoted in Unruh, *The Plains Across,* p. 111.
37. Quoted in Eaton, *The Overland Trail,* p. 10.

Chapter 3: How They Got There

38. Quoted in Schlissel, *Women's Diaries,* p. 38.
39. Quoted in Fanselow, *The Traveler's Guide,* p. 182.
40. Quoted in Paden, *The Wake of the Prairie Schooner,* p. 268.
41. Quoted in Eaton, *The Overland Trail,* pp. 26, 27.
42. Quoted in Eaton, *The Overland Trail,* pp. 28–29.
43. Quoted in Editors of Time-Life Books, *The Pioneers,* p. 48.
44. Palmer, *Journal of Travels,* p. 144.
45. Quoted in Dale Morgan, ed., *Overland in 1846: Diaries and Letters of the California-Oregon Trail.* Lincoln: University of Nebraska Press, 1963, pp. 482–83.
46. Marcy, *The Prairie Traveler,* p. 15.
47. Palmer, *Journal of Travels,* pp. 43–44.
48. Quoted in Morgan, *Overland in 1846,* p. 586.
49. Quoted in Morgan, *Overland in 1846,* p. 570.
50. Quoted in Morgan, *Overland in 1846,* p. 634–35.
51. Quoted in Unruh, *The Plains Across,* p. 123.
52. Masterson, *One Woman's West,* p. 41.
53. Quoted in Unruh, *The Plains Across,* p. 133.
54. Quoted in Unruh, *The Plains Across,* p. 134.
55. Quoted in Unruh, *The Plains Across,* p. 132.
56. Quoted in Unruh, *The Plains Across,* p. 137.

Chapter 4: How a Wagon Train Worked

57. Quoted in Unruh, *The Plains Across,* p. 119.
58. Quoted in Eaton, *The Overland Trail,* pp. 86, 153.
59. Quoted in Schlissel, *Women's Diaries,* p. 172.
60. Quoted in Morgan, *Overland in 1846,* pp. 557–58.
61. Quoted in Hewitt, *Eye-Witnesses,* pp. 42–43.
62. Marcy, *The Prairie Traveler,* p. 183.
63. Quoted in Hewitt, *Eye-Witnesses,* p. 58.
64. Quoted in Eaton, *The Overland Trail,* p. 43.
65. Quoted in Eaton, *The Overland Trail,* pp. 59–60.
66. Quoted in Editors of Time-Life Books, *The Pioneers,* pp. 92–93.
67. Quoted in Morgan, *Overland in 1846,* p. 557.
68. Quoted in Schlissel, *Women's Diaries,* p. 39.
69. Quoted in Judith E. Greenberg and Helen Carey McKeever, *A Pioneer Woman's Memoir: Based on the Journal of Arabella Clemens Fulton.* New York: Franklin Watts, 1995, p. 42.

70. Quoted in Schlissel, *Women's Diaries*, p. 84.
71. Quoted in Eaton, *The Overland Trail*, p. 43.
72. Marcy, *The Prairie Traveler*, pp. 56, 59.
73. Quoted in Schlissel, *Women's Diaries*, p. 172.
74. Quoted in Eaton, *The Overland Trail*, p. 91.
75. Quoted in Hewitt, *Eye-Witnesses*, p. 57.
76. Quoted in Schlissel, *Women's Diaries*, p. 175.

Chapter 5: How They Coped

77. Quoted in Schlissel, *Women's Diaries*, p. 83.
78. Quoted in Schlissel, *Women's Diaries*, pp. 82–83.
79. Quoted in Greenberg and McKeever, *A Pioneer Woman's Memoir*, p. 87.
80. Quoted in Schlissel, *Women's Diaries*, pp. 80–81.
81. Quoted in Eaton, *The Overland Trail*, p. 116.
82. Quoted in Eaton, *The Overland Trail*, p. 187.
83. Quoted in Eaton, *The Overland Trail*, p. 88.
84. Quoted in Eaton, *The Overland Trail*, p. 137.
85. Quoted in Morgan, *Overland in 1846*, p. 561.
86. Quoted in Morgan, *Overland in 1846*, p. 565.
87. Quoted in David Lavender, *Westward Vision: The Story of the Oregon Trail*. New York: McGraw-Hill, 1963, p. 295.
88. Quoted in Morgan, *Overland in 1846*, p. 612.
89. Quoted in Eaton, *The Overland Trail*, p. 159.
90. Palmer, *Journal of Travels*, p. 143.
91. Quoted in Hewitt, *Eye-Witnesses*, p. 16.
92. Palmer, *Journal of Travels*, p. 34.
93. Quoted in Unruh, *The Plains Across*, p. 386.
94. Quoted in Editors of Time-Life Books, *The Pioneers*, p. 107.
95. Quoted in Eaton, *The Overland Trail*, p. 88.
96. Francis Parkman, *The Oregon Trail: Sketches of Prairie and Rocky-Mountain Life*. Williamstown, MA: Corner House, 1980, p. 67.
97. Quoted in Eaton, *The Overland Trail*, p. 180.
98. Quoted in Eaton, *The Overland Trail*, p. 98.
99. Quoted in Eaton, *The Overland Trail*, p. 128.
100. Quoted in Paden, *The Wake of the Prairie Schooner*, p. 269.
101. Quoted in Greenberg and McKeever, *A Pioneer Woman's Memoir*, pp. 37–38.
102. Quoted in Morgan, *Overland in 1846*, pp. 553–54.
103. Quoted in Unruh, *The Plains Across*, p. 414.

Chapter 6: How They Interacted with the Indians

104. Masterson, *One Woman's West*, p. 25.
105. Masterson, *One Woman's West*, p. 48.
106. Palmer, *Journal of Travels*, p. 17.
107. Parkman, *The Oregon Trail*, p. 30.
108. Paden, *The Wake of the Prairie Schooner*, p. 42.
109. Parkman, *The Oregon Trail*, p. 70.
110. Palmer, *Journal of Travels*, p. 27.
111. Quoted in Unruh, *The Plains Across*, p. 160.
112. Masterson, *One Woman's West*, p. 36.
113. Palmer, *Journal of Travels*, p. 54.
114. Palmer, *Journal of Travels*, p. 54.
115. Masterson, *One Woman's West*, p. 50.
116. Masterson, *One Woman's West*, pp. 29–30.

117. Masterson, *One Woman's West,* p. 36.

118. Quoted in Schlissel, *Women's Diaries,* pp. 118–19.

119. Quoted in Unruh, *The Plains Across,* p. 162.

120. Quoted in Hewitt, *Eye-Witnesses,* pp. 66, 68.

121. Quoted in Greenberg and McKeever, *A Pioneer Woman's Memoir,* pp. 69–71.

122. Masterson, *One Woman's West,* p. 37.

123. Quoted in Eaton, *The Overland Trail,* p. 37.

124. Quoted in Morgan, *Overland in 1846,* p. 167.

125. Quoted in Hewitt, *Eye-Witnesses,* p. 147.

126. Quoted in Morgan, *Overland in 1846,* p. 574.

127. Quoted in Eaton, *The Overland Trail,* pp. 77–78.

128. Quoted in Schlissel, *Women's Diaries,* p. 133.

129. Marcy, *The Prairie Traveler,* p. 198.

130. Quoted in Morgan, *Overland in 1846,* p. 584.

131. Palmer, *Journal of Travels,* p. 144.

132. Quoted in Schlissel, *Women's Diaries,* pp. 222, 224.

Chapter 7: How They Came to Grief

133. Quoted in Morgan, *Overland in 1846,* p. 152.

134. Quoted in Paden, *The Wake of the Prairie Schooner,* p. 33.

135. Masterson, *One Woman's West,* p. 30.

136. Quoted in Eaton, *The Overland Trail,* pp. 119–20.

137. Quoted in Schlissel, *Women's Diaries,* p. 212.

138. Quoted in Schlissel, *Women's Diaries,* p. 49.

139. Quoted in Unruh, *The Plains Across,* p. 412.

140. Quoted in Paden, *The Wake of the Prairie Schooner,* p. 4.

141. Marcy, *The Prairie Traveler,* p. 171.

142. Quoted in Unruh, *The Plains Across,* p. 413.

143. Quoted in Schlissel, *Women's Diaries,* p. 103.

144. Quoted in Eaton, *The Overland Trail,* p. 71.

145. Quoted in Paden, *The Wake of the Prairie Schooner,* pp. 192–93.

146. Quoted in Eaton, *The Overland Trail,* p. 30.

147. Quoted in Schlissel, *Women's Diaries,* p. 211.

148. Quoted in Schlissel, *Women's Diaries,* pp. 129–30.

149. Quoted in Schlissel, *Women's Diaries,* p. 69.

150. Marcy, *The Prairie Traveler,* p. 125.

151. Quoted in Eaton, *The Overland Trail,* p. 167.

152. Quoted in Eaton, *The Overland Trail,* pp. 41–42.

153. Quoted in Schlissel, *Women's Diaries,* p. 59.

154. Quoted in Eaton, *The Overland Trail,* p. 104.

155. Quoted in Schlissel, *Women's Diaries,* p. 59.

156. Quoted in Arthur King Peters, *Seven Trails West.* New York: Abbeville Press, 1996, pp. 97–98.

157. Quoted in Eaton, *The Overland Trail,* pp. 138–39.

158. Quoted in Schlissel, *Women's Diaries,* p. 47.

159. Quoted in Eaton, *The Overland Trail,* p. 165.

160. Quoted in Eaton, *The Overland Trail,* p. 118.

161. Quoted in Eaton, *The Overland Trail,*

p. 56.

162. Quoted in Eaton, *The Overland Trail*, p. 173.

Chapter 8: What They Found to Enjoy

163. Quoted in Eaton, *The Overland Trail*, p. 152.
164. Quoted in Eaton, *The Overland Trail*, pp. 123–24.
165. Quoted in Morgan, *Overland in 1846*, p. 615.
166. Quoted in Eaton, *The Overland Trail*, p. 62.
167. Quoted in Eaton, *The Overland Trail*, p. 106.
168. Quoted in Hewitt, *Eye-Witnesses*, pp. 61–62.
169. Quoted in Hewitt, *Eye-Witnesses*, p. 60.
170. Quoted in Eaton, *The Overland Trail*, pp. 168–70.
171. Quoted in Eaton, *The Overland Trail*, p. 160.
172. Quoted in Morgan, *Overland in 1846*, p. 608.
173. Quoted in Eaton, *The Overland Trail*, p. 231.
174. Quoted in Paden, *The Wake of the Prairie Schooner*, p. 275.
175. Quoted in Paden, *The Wake of the Prairie Schooner*, p. 275.
176. Quoted in Fanselow, *The Traveler's Guide*, p. 128.
177. Palmer, *Journal of Travels*, p. 39.
178. Quoted in Schlissel, *Women's Diaries*, p. 180.
179. Quoted in Morgan, *Overland in 1846*, p. 555.
180. Quoted in Schlissel, *Women's Diaries*, p. 66.
181. Masterson, *One Woman's West*, p. 35.
182. Quoted in Schlissel, *Women's Diaries*, p. 222.
183. Quoted in Eaton, *The Overland Trail*, p. 78.
184. Quoted in Hewitt, *Eye-Witnesses*, p. 57.
185. Quoted in Eaton, *The Overland Trail*, pp. 109–11.
186. Quoted in Eaton, *The Overland Trail*, pp. 111–12.
187. Palmer, *Journal of Travels*, p. 35.
188. Masterson, *One Woman's West*, p. 52.
189. Quoted in Schlissel, *Women's Diaries*, p. 148.
190. Quoted in Lavender, *Westward Vision*, pp. 392–93.
191. Quoted in Morgan, *Overland in 1846*, p. 685.
192. Quoted in Lavender, *Westward Vision*, p. 392.
193. Masterson, *One Woman's West*, p. 59.

Epilogue: The End of the Trail

194. Quoted in Editors of Time-Life Books, *The Trailblazers*, p. 162.
195. Quoted in Eaton, *The Overland Trail*, p. 45.

For Further Reading

Dayton Duncan, *The West: An Illustrated History for Children*. Boston: Little, Brown, 1996.

————, *People of the West*. Boston: Little, Brown, 1996.

Liza Ketchum, *The Gold Rush*. Boston: Little, Brown, 1996. These three titles are companion volumes to the PBS series *The West*. All are well written and filled with photographs and black-and-white reproductions of paintings.

Editors of American Heritage, *Westward on the Oregon Trail*. New York: American Heritage, 1962. A lavishly illustrated history of the trail, from the days of the fur trappers to the advent of the stagecoach and the Pony Express.

Suzanne Hilton, *Getting There: Frontier Travel Without Power*. Philadelphia: Westminster Press, 1980. A fascinating survey of the various methods of transportation on the frontier, from ships to stagecoaches to covered wagons. Quotes from nineteenth-century travelers are sprinkled throughout.

Glen Rounds, *The Prairie Schooners*. New York: Holiday House, 1968. A brief, readable look at life in a covered wagon, accompanied by drawings in Rounds's trademark humorous, sketchy style.

Rebecca Stefoff, *Children of the Westward Trail*. Brookfield, CT: Millbrook Press, 1996. A simple overview of the overland experience that emphasizes what it was like for children.

Major Works Consulted

Herbert Eaton, *The Overland Trail to California in 1852*. New York: Putnam's, 1974. A collection of brief excerpts from the diaries of dozens of men and women who headed west in a single year. Some of the selections consist of one sentence, some of several pages. They are in chronological order, so the reader gets a clear picture of how the trail and the emigrants themselves changed as the train moved from east to west.

Julie Fanselow, *The Traveler's Guide to the Oregon Trail*. Helena, MT: Falcon Press, 1992. A useful handbook for those interested in retracing all or part of the trail route. The book describes dozens of historic sites along the trail, plus some interesting side trips, and briefly relates the history behind them.

James Hewitt, ed., *Eye-Witnesses to Wagon Trains West*. New York: Scribner's, 1973. Selections from the diaries of emigrants who participated in five different episodes in the trail's history: the first wagon train (1841), the Great Emigration of 1843, the Donner party, the Mormon emigration, and the California gold rush. Jesse Applegate's diary (1843) is especially literate.

David Lavender, *Westward Vision: The Story of the Oregon Trail*. New York: McGraw-Hill, 1963. Only a small part of the book deals with the emigrants, but it does offer a very complete and readable history of the early explorers and their efforts to find an easy route to the Pacific.

Randolph B. Marcy, *The Prairie Traveler: A Hand-Book for Overland Expeditions*. Williamstown, MA: Corner House, 1968. Unlike Palmer's and Farnham's guidebooks, this is not an account of a single trip west but a manual designed to give emigrants as much advice as possible about trail travel. The prose is stiff and the information often seems aimed at soldiers rather than civilians, but the book is comprehensive and detailed.

Martha Gay Masterson, *One Woman's West: Recollections of the Oregon Trail and Settling the Northwest Country*. Ed. Lois Barton. Eugene, OR: Spencer Butte Press, 1986. A memoir written forty years after Martha Gay's family traveled the Oregon Trail. Only three chapters deal with the actual journey, but they give valuable insight into the feelings and concerns of an ordinary young girl faced with a new and sometimes frightening experience.

Dale Morgan, ed., *Overland in 1846: Diaries and Letters of the California-Oregon Trail*. Lincoln: University of Nebraska Press, 1963. Two volumes of complete letters and diary entries, printed with the original, often odd, grammar and spelling and punctuation—or lack of it. One of the best sources of unedited material.

Irene D. Paden, *The Wake of the Prairie Schooner*. New York, Macmillan, 1947. A classic on the history of the trail, first published in 1943. Well written and full of humorous anecdotes, about both the emigrants' experiences and Paden's own experiences retracing the route of the trail.

Joel Palmer, *Journal of Travels over the Rocky Mountains*. Ann Arbor, MI: University Microfilms, 1966. Partly an account of Palmer's 1845 trip west and partly a guidebook for other emigrants that includes a table of distances, a description of Oregon Country, and a vocabulary of Chinook and Nez Percé words.

Francis Parkman, *The Oregon Trail: Sketches of Prairie and Rocky-Mountain Life.* Williamstown, MA: Corner House, 1980. The most famous of all books about the trail, first published in 1847. Parkman is entertaining but subjective, and more concerned with the Indians he encounters than with his fellow overlanders.

Lillian Schlissel, *Women's Diaries of the Westward Journey.* New York: Schocken, 1982. Schlissel draws on the diaries of ninety-six women emigrants to give a picture of trail life from a female perspective. About two-thirds of the book is Schlissel's overview of the experience, illustrated with quotes from emigrant diaries; the other third consists of lengthy segments from four representative diaries.

John D. Unruh Jr., *The Plains Across: The Overland Emigrants and the Trans-Mississippi West, 1840–60.* Urbana: University of Illinois Press, 1979. Unruh's doctoral dissertation is thoroughly researched and scholarly but also quite readable. The book focuses on how emigrants interacted with one another, with Indians, and with entrepreneurs. Full of facts and figures and details not available in other books about the trail.

Additional Works Consulted

Malcolm Clark Jr., *Eden Seekers: The Settlement of Oregon, 1818–1862.* Boston: Houghton Mifflin, 1981.

Bernard DeVoto, *Across the Wide Missouri.* Boston: Houghton Mifflin, 1947.

Dayton Duncan, *Lewis & Clark: The Journey of the Corps of Discovery.* New York: Knopf, 1997.

Editors of Time-Life Books, *The Pioneers.* New York: Time-Life, 1974.

————, *The Trailblazers.* New York: Time-Life, 1973.

Thomas J. Farnham, *Travels in the Great Western Prairies, the Anahuac and Rocky Mountains, and in the Oregon Territory.* New York: Da Capo Press, 1973.

Gregory M. Franzwa, *The Oregon Trail Revisited.* St. Louis: Patrice Press, 1972.

Judith E. Greenberg and Helen Carey McKeever, *A Pioneer Woman's Memoir: Based on the Journal of Arabella Clemens Fulton.* New York: Franklin Watts, 1995.

David Lavender, *The Fist in the Wilderness.* Garden City, NY: Doubleday, 1964.

Arthur King Peters, *Seven Trails West.* New York: Abbeville Press, 1996.

Gerald S. Snyder, *In the Footsteps of Lewis & Clark.* Washington, DC: National Geographic Society, 1970.

Special Publications Division, National Geographic Society, *Trails West.* Washington, DC: National Geographic Society, 1979.

George R. Stewart, *The California Trail: An Epic with Many Heroes.* Lincoln: University of Nebraska Press, 1962.

Geoffrey C. Ward, *The West: An Illustrated History.* Boston: Little, Brown, 1996.

Index

Picture Credits

About the Author

Gary L. Blackwood is a playwright, novelist, and nonfiction writer. He writes for adult and children's magazines on a wide range of subjects but specializes in history and biography. Many of his plays and novels are set in the past, from the twelfth century to the 1960s. His nonfiction books include a biography of Theodore Roosevelt and a series that explores paranormal phenomena (ghosts, ESP, UFOs, reincarnation, etc.). He and his wife and two children live in the country near Carthage, Missouri.

DATE DUE		
SEP 3 0 2001		
MAR 1 0 200%		
NOV 0 3 2005		
GAYLORD		PRINTED IN U.S.A.